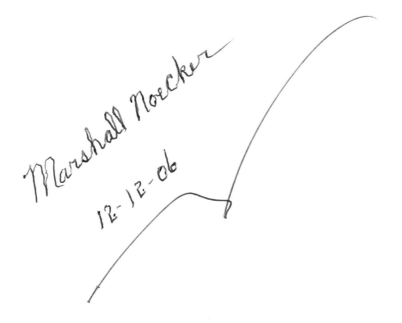

Marshall Noecker
12-12-06

READ FIRST
INTRODUCTION AND TESTIMONIAL

HE WENT EAST
AND
HE DONE GOOD

MARSHALL NOECKER

HE WENT EAST

AND

HE DONE GOOD

Sanborn Press
Grosse Pointe Farms, Michigan

Published by Sanborn Press
33 Warner Road
Grosse Pointe Farms, Michigan 48236

Publisher's Cataloging-in-Publication Data
Noecker, Marshall.
    He went east and he done good / Marshall Noecker – Grosse Pointe
    Farms, Mich: Sanborn Press, 2000.
        p.   cm.
    ISBN 0-9671663-0-6
    1. Noecker, Marshall.   2. Frontier and pioneer life—North Dakota.
    3. North Dakota—History—Biography. I. Title.
F655 .N65   2000   99-90341
978.4'02   [B]—dc21   CIP

PROJECT COORDINATION BY JENKINS GROUP, INC.

04 03 02 01 00 ◆ 5 4 3 2 1

Printed in the United States of America

This book is dedicated to my family.
My darling wife, Sandra

Our children:
Marshall R. Noecker
Ann Noecker Dawson
William I Noecker
Nancy Noecker Debosek
Richard J. Spangler
Gregory E. Spangler
Nicholas A. Noecker
Alexandra Noecker Ferrara

My co-workers:
David J. Padilla
Robert I. Smith
Kenneth Thom
Robert V. Yazejian
Glenn Hustead
George Gazepis

Contents

Preface

WHAT A GREAT LIFE, AND THANKS TO GOOD HEALTH, IT GOES ON AND ON.

Back in 1981 when it was popular to build up one's family trees, I fell into the mode of the times and researched and wrote two books on my family. The first was a story on my Mother's side going back to 1754 in Germany. The second was a research of my Father's family going back to 1750, also in Germany.

Over the nearly twenty years since these two endeavors, a lot of friends have apparently enjoyed reading and studying my writing. These friends have encouraged me to put my life in a book. So here it is.

Pictures have always been a large part of my life, and so I have included a wide selection to help identify my life... past and present. Particularly in my early years, photos were not common and therefore I have to rely on words and a few pictures to tell my story.

My story begins in the prairies of North Dakota. All four of my grandparents had arrived on the plains only about thirty-five years previous to my birth, and therefore my early years were colored with a lot of European background. Some of the many characteristics of my mind, my body, and my actions can be traced back to the "old country."

I could have stayed back on the north and western land, but for some unknown reason I was motivated to move on. Thank goodness I was also born with a competitive spirit. I wanted to have the best, to be the leader, and to achieve. Yet I recognized that every action must be followed by a reaction. As you succeed you must be careful not to leave any crushed feelings in your wake.

I am now eighty-two years old, and therefore this story covers nearly eighty years of memory. Many of the events have been omitted because they have been forgotten to the passing of time. Other events may have been colored for the same reason. As the years go by, probably the facts get mingled. It is like the old game where twenty people sit in a circle and start a sentence around the group. By the time it makes the rounds, we do not recognize the final sentence compared to the original words.

I have used the actual names of a lot of people, living and dead, and in many cases have their verbal approval. However, in those cases where I haven't told them of my story, I hope they will be happy and pleased to recognize that I could not have written this story of my life without including them.

This is a story of my life. It if accomplishes no more than a history of my actions for my children, grandchildren and their descendants, I will have met my goals.

Acknowledgments

BARBARA ZEBROWSKI — FOR HER CONTINUED SUPPORT, ENCOURAGEMENT and dedication to this manuscript. She is responsible for this book. My family will love her for the history.

Nikki Stahl — for her successful dedication to turning these four hundred pages of double-spaced, typewritten story into a masterful book.

Theresa Nelson — for leading and directing this program to the finish. When we got off track she always brought us back to the goal.

Introduction

IN EVERYONE'S LIFE THERE MUST COME A TIME WHEN A PERSON WONDERS what are the features of life that were responsible for his conception, birth, and successful childhood. My paternal grandparents, Leo and Amelia Noecker, wanted ten children — living. Little Amelia was born in 1880. She was their tenth living child. Mission accomplished.

However, four years later, little Amelia died suddenly. Since Dakota territory was in the process of being inhabited there was no undertaker, no preacher, no cemetery, and very few neighbors close enough in distance to lend much family support. The story has been told and retold.

My grandfather built a coffin from scraps of wood found on the farm. Grandmother washed the body and clothed it in the best undergarments and dress that she had available.

Where should the burial be? My grandfather, in his mind, surveyed his land. He settled on a hillside facing west and dug the grave. The story goes that my grandfather acted as the preacher and gave a moving Lutheran sermon for little Amelia. Her nine brothers and sisters each gave their memories and prayers for Amelia. They named the cemetery "Fairview."

Leo and Amelia decided they would and could have another baby to round out their mission of ten living children. My dad, William, was born twelve months later. And that is why I'm here today.

I remind my blood descendents of this story often, and today I count up the people who are on this earth due to the untimely death of Amelia Noecker at four years of age. At least thirty-some people survive. My sister with four children and twelve grandchildren. My brother with two children. And in my case, eight children and nine grandchildren.

And this is my story...

HE WENT EAST

AND

HE DONE GOOD

Arriving in the Dakota Territory

MOST AMERICANS KNOW LITTLE ABOUT THEIR FAMILY HISTORY. IN MY case I became very interested in genealogy in the late 1970's when Alex Haley wrote Roots. This story inspired me to research both of my parents' families back to 1750 Germany.

Karl Ludwig Caspary Nocker was born on March 30, 1800 in Schmallenberg, Westphalia, Germany. Great-grandmother Johanne Friederike Wilhelmine Schneider was born on March 10, 1803 in Finsterwalse, Brandernberg, Prussia. They were married on September 14, 1823 and had five sons and five daughters.

Eight of the children were born from July 28, 1824 to January 14, 1834 and were baptized with the surname Nocker. When Emma and (my grandfather) Leo Ernst were born, their surname was recorded as Noecker.

Two reasons for the name change. First, my ancestors had settled along the Neckar River in Germany. As with typical stories of history, my ancestors became closely related to the river and took some form of its name as their own, which provided a direct relationship between the river and my ancestors.

Additionally, Ludwig was evidently a very enterprising business man and constructed a series of livery stables and hotels across Germany with the western terminal in Alsace Lorraine on the French Border. Ludwig wanted a "French connection" and added the "e".

Since the first eight children were minors when the "e" was added, they all went through a name change, making all the surnames "Noecker."

Ludwig operated his livery stables and hotels successfully until 1856. As the tale goes, a Russian power invaded Germany from the East and determined that Ludwig's property should be theirs. They took him into custody, and the next day delivered his body to his family claiming that he committed suicide. Of course his family knew that this was not true because strict Lutherans saw suicide as a crime against the church.

Wilhelmine knew she had to take action before her five sons fell to the same fate. Luckily, she had enough money to book passage for herself, her five sons, and two unmarried daughters to Canada.

In 1880 my grandfather, Leo Noecker, the youngest of Wilhelmine's ten children, heard of land available in Dakota Territory through grants from the Northern Pacific Railroad. When the railroad went through this new territory, the federal government gave them every other mile on each side of the track, one mile wide and twenty miles deep. As you can see, this made a checkerboard pattern of railroad land on either side of the track. The federal government owned the strips of land between the grants to the railroad, and Grandfather Noecker made a request for a strip of the government land. The grant came through and the original transfer of title to my grandfather was signed by Grover Cleveland, president of the U.S. I have the title.

Within a few months, Grandfather Noecker, his wife, and eight children arrived in Valley City, Dakota Territory. They rented a horse and wagon to make the twelve-mile trek to their new piece of land. At about the same time, Mother's parents, Augustus Brock and his wife,

Julianna, were granted a piece of land by the U.S. Government five miles down the railroad track and on the same side.

Of course, at that time, neither family knew the other.

Gustav Brock, who was Mother's father, was born in West Freisen, Germany, on August 27, 1854. Julianna Hoeft, my maternal grandmother, came to Dearborn, Michigan, with her parents in 1873. She was seventeen years old.

In 1878 my maternal grandparents moved to Dakota Territory, where they took up a homestead adjoining Gustav's half brother, Henry, and his family. Ten years later, the federal government issued them Homestead Certificate #2612, signed by President Grover Cleveland, which gave them ownership of their land.

To this union eight children were born, the last two being twins. The oldest, William, was born in Michigan. He left Dakota at an early age for Montana, where he married an Indian Princess, the Chief's daughter.

Gustav built a sod house where he, Julianna, and little William spent their first year. When Julianna's parents heard of the poorly constructed home their daughter was living in, they boarded a train to save her.

Upon their arrival, my great-grandfather designed a two-room house. He bought the lumber and had it delivered forty miles by two horse teams. With the help of his wife, son-in-law, and daughter, he spent the summer building the house. When completed, Julianna's parents returned to Ypsilanti where they spent the rest of their lives.

Then in the early 1900s my grandparents on my mother's side accumulated enough money to build a large, four bedroom farmhouse for their family. They transformed the old house into a seed shed, where my cousin and I often played later in our childhood.

T w o

My Early Years

I WAS BORN IN NORTH DAKOTA IN 1915, IN MY GRANDFATHER'S STONE house. There were two-foot-wide windowsills on the first and second floors where all of the grandchildren enjoyed playing, resting, or sleeping as the sun shone in to keep us warm.

My earliest memory goes back to approximately four years of age. We had a brown horse called Dolly that my six-year-old sister was riding bareback. In accordance with the rules of most ranchers and farmers, all little kids learned to ride bareback, so if they fell, slipped, or were bucked off, they would not get caught in the saddle. I remember Adeline riding down the road, and me, with a cap in my hand, trying to scare the horse. I finally succeeded when I threw my cap at the animal's head and old Dolly took off at a gallop toward the barn. Father was nearby, and when he saw the horse running toward the open barn door, he took off like lightning and caught the bridle just before the horse entered. Obviously Adeline would have been knocked off by hitting the overhead barn door, but when Father grabbed the reins, she fell into his arms.

Early school time brought my next memory. I was in the first grade and there were twenty kids in my class. About half of them were girls, which were my chief interest.

We had a traditional rural school with two classes in each room. The first and second grades were in one, while third and fourth, fifth and sixth, and seventh and eighth grades were in others. The high school was housed on the second floor.

Our desks were wide enough for two people. When the teacher got the first grade together for reading, the second grade had to sit on one side and study. Although I think they often found other things to do.

I always wanted to sit with one of the girls — Helen Snider — whom I found infatuating. Often I would push the other kids out of the way to get to her. She was my first attraction and I honestly believe she received more of my attention than my studies did.

This infatuation only lasted a year until I met a new girl, Jean Raye Bassett. She moved into the community when her father was assigned to run the local bank.

One evening I did not come home from school, and when darkness approached Father and Mother became frantic. Jean Raye had invited me to her home where we shared lunch and played for most of the day. It didn't occur to any of us, except Mother, that I needed to get home before dark. After that, Mother and the teacher agreed that I should sit with only boys in the class.

In fourth grade we learned the ABCs (which I must have learned several years before), and how to write. Writing class was considered a curriculum topic, much like arithmetic, English, and reading. The technique used to teach us was called Palmer Writing. Around the room, at the top of the blackboard, the teacher placed examples of every letter of the alphabet shown in three categories: the small letter, the capital letter, and the script letter. There were also many different-sized circles that we used to help us with our handwriting. By following these circles, we were expected to write legibly.

We also had the multiplication tables, and I was an expert on the multiplication of everything through the number twelve. From then on, we used the principle of the abacus. This principle is based on multiplying everything by ten and adding specific numbers. This is how I learned to figure in my head that twenty-three times twenty-two equals five hundred and six.

Father and Mother were always interested in teaching us kids the little they knew about the world. I have always felt that Father should have been an educator instead of a farmer. He spent so much time teaching us numbers, geography, and English. When he would milk the cows, he would ask me questions like, "What is the capital of Montana?" I am sure it is because of this, that I could recite the capital of every state in the union by the time I was ten.

The fourth grade ended in tragedy for our school. At the end of the school year, the kids were always taken in an old bus, on a ten-mile trip to the place where the Cheyenne River flowed through our area. The water was fast-moving due to the melting of the snow and ice. Father and Mother did not let Adeline, my brother Ray, or I attend this picnic because they thought the river was dangerous. They knew what they were talking about, because my lovely teacher, Florence Bennett, drowned in the river on that picnic day.

When I entered the fifth grade, we had many new children in our school. My interests were again absorbed in the girls of the class. The Carpenter twins, Leona and Leola, now replaced the girls of the past.

I think up until this time I had enjoyed the company of Helen, Charlotte, and Marian by sitting close to them or playing with the same toy. However, with the Carpenter twins it was different. In fifth grade, boys begin to realize that girls bodies are different than theirs. And the thought of touching them really set off a new line of interest.

My teacher was a lovely young lady named Evelyn Alfson. Her home was in Binford, North Dakota, which was about fifty miles up a spur railroad track off the North Pacific Railroad. My teacher would tell us of her experience riding this spur train, first to Sanborn, then switching to the main line for the twelve-mile ride to Valley City where she attended the North Dakota State Teachers College. After completing her teaching degree, she was hired as our fifth-grade teacher.

There were seven to eight stops on this fifty-mile run, and the train made it daily, up and back. No one had ever heard of an eight-hour work day at that time, and the train would set out at daybreak and return after dark. On the way, it would pick up eggs, cream, milk, and butter from the farmers. The larger cars would be left at certain stations, and after a few days would be loaded with wheat, barley, or oats to be hauled down to the main line and moved into the Minnesota or Chicago markets.

These trains usually consisted of about six boxcars, a mail car, and a coach car for passengers. In the mail car, mail was picked up at each stop, sorted, and left off at the appropriate stop.

In 1921 electricity came to North Dakota and ran parallel to High-way 10, which was the first surveyed road across the state. Highway 10 was nothing more than a strip of land about twenty feet wide and graded with dirt. When the spring and fall rains came, this road was a mire of mud. The cars that traversed the road ran the risk of getting stuck to the point that it was impossible for the driver to get off without assistance. Since this road bisected our land, these travelers would often come to our house for help. Father made sure our two-horse teams and hired hands were always ready to pull out a stranded automobile.

Father, always a progressive person, negotiated to have power brought to our home. "I would like to have electricity run to my farm," he explained. The Ottertail Power Company agreed on the terms that Father would run the electric poles and supply the wire from the main road to our farm, then they would hook up the electricity. I can still remember the first night we had an electric light bulb extended into our kitchen. What a thrill it was for my family to be the first in this rural North Dakota territory to have this luxury!

Father and Mother had a Sears Roebuck and Co. catalog from which they ordered electric fixtures, switches, and plugs for our new, modern home. During the winter months, Father and a "North Dakota Mechanic" ran the wires across the attic and down into the various rooms with one big light fixture hanging down in the center and a string to turn it on and off. Our neighbors would come from miles around just to pull the string and marvel at the new technology.

Naturally, when the electricity came in, that did not mean the end of the kerosene lamps. We had been told that electricity was subject to breaks in the service and there might be minutes, hours, and even days when the Ottertail Power Company would be plagued by interruptions. Therefore, Father and Mother kept all the kerosene lamps in service.

One evening, while sitting under one of these lamps, the glass chimney cracked into dozens of pieces, one which made its way to my bare arm, causing a severe cut between my wrist and elbow. Our family was nearly a hundred miles from the nearest doctor, so Father and Mother had to provide all the medical attention. First, they tied a tourniquet around my arm, just above the elbow, to stop the bleeding. Although there was always the fear that if left on too long, the tourniquet would cause a loss of function in the arm or hand.

All that night, Father and Mother took turns holding the cut together, helping the blood to coagulate. As I recall, each would take a half hour pushing their thumb into the cut. Miraculously, in the morning the cut had sealed itself. A light band-aid was put over it, and my arm placed in a sling until it was healed completely.

That summer, another small catastrophe occurred. On a windy day, the door from our kitchen leading into the living room blew shut, catching the tip of my thumb in the jamb. I let out the biggest yell of my life as the end of my thumb fell to the floor. Mother ran over, grabbed the tip of my thumb in one cloth and the remainder of the thumb in another, and led me down the street to the local barber.

The barber lived about a half mile away and was the closest thing we had to a surgeon. He placed the cut off end of my thumb back where it belonged, dabbed it with dark brown iodine, and wrapped it in a swab to make the biggest dumbbell I've ever seen. He instructed Mother to soak the bandage in iodine for several days, then bring me in for another look.

One week later we returned, and to everyone's surprise, the end of my thumb had reattached itself! (However, today I have one thumb that is a quarter inch shorter than the other.)

When I was six years old, Father bought a new, four-runner sleigh from the Sears catalog. We used it to go to Mother's parents' house for Thanksgiving. A grain box, about three and a half foot wide, three foot tall, and twelve foot long was placed on the sled for us to ride in. Because it seemed to be an especially cold and snowy Thanksgiving, Father hitched the wildest team of horses, loaded my mother, brother, sister, and me into the box, and away we went.

Also arriving at our grandparents' house were Mother's two sisters and their children. The families were each given one of the rooms in the house, with my grandparents taking the fourth. I remember sleeping on the floor where Mother would wrap us in blankets to keep us warm. It was a great time to whoop it up with our cousins!

At this time I remember our family experiences with the Sioux and the Mandan Indians. The Indians would follow the trails through our land as they migrated to the east in the winter and the west in the summer. There would be a group of about ten families who rode horses, with the squaws being the most colorful part of their caravans. My siblings and I were not allowed to use the word "squaw" because our parents thought it was degrading. Instead, they instructed us to call them "mother."

In each family, the mother had a pony with two long sticks tied to the pony's back and the ends dragging on the ground. In this little area, about two feet wide between the poles, they would have their tents, cooking utensils, and all their other worldly possessions. Because we had a lot of horses, the Indians loved to trade with us. In most of the trades, Father felt that the Indians had taken advantage of him by walking off with one of his good horses, while he accepted a miserable one in return. We found that it was very difficult to judge the value of a horse by its appearance. Some of the best-looking horses were the most miserable to work.

Once we had a beautiful brown horse with a white blaze that we got in trade. Father hitched him up with three other horses to pull a grain binder. To everyone's surprise, this big, beautiful horse looked at the binder behind him and laid down in the middle of the field. The men tried to get him up to do his job, but with no success. When he finally arose, he stood looking defiantly at the men as if to say, "I will not work." This must be where the phrase "IWW (I Won't Work) membership" came from!

What happened to this beautiful horse? When the next small tribe of

Indians came through the area, he was traded for a skinny, mouse-colored horse, who turned out to be an excellent worker. We learned that in most cases, the skinny horse, with some good hay and oats, grew much larger and stronger, and more capable of handling the work than the pretty horses. We will never know what happened to the beautiful, brown horse, but we are sure some farmer down the line went through the same experience that Father did.

The difference between the Indian kids and us was that they were dressed in all leather, where we wore mostly wool. We would try to trade clothes with them, because we thought they were more colorfully dressed than us in our plain, old, wool clothes. We especially liked the beads, trinkets, and stones, which hung from their shirts and dresses.

As I grew older and entered high school, there were several Indian girls that joined our student body. One in particular was Alyce La France. Alyce was a girl with dark hair, a beautiful face, and a passable figure. In one of the school plays I was the young farm boy and Alyce was a young farm girl from a neighboring homestead. We carried on a romance that was supposed to produce results to the satisfaction of both farm families down the road. When Mother found out about the play and its consequences of joining two big farms together, and the fact that I was the hero and Alyce was the heroine, she had many sleepless nights. Her biggest fear was that I would either marry Alyce, or Alyce would get pregnant. Which she thought would come first — I do not know.

What do North Dakota kids do during the long winter months for entertainment? Make ice cream.

Every farm family had a one-gallon ice cream freezer. An ice cream freezer was a large, wooden bucket which held a metal container about five inches in diameter and sixteen inches tall, with a beater inside. Over the top was a crank mechanism which you turned with your elbow grease.

Milk, cream, and ice were readily available. The mixture was made of cream, milk, eggs, sugar, baking soda, cornstarch, and vanilla extract. All you needed to do was find a cake of ice, chip it up, and put it around the freezer. It took about a half hour of continuous turning before the ice cream formed. Then we would let it settle for another half hour before the ice cream social. Many of the neighbor kids would stay the night after making ice cream.

We also got into cooking other dishes, and visualized ourselves as gourmet chefs. Apple and tapioca puddings were other favorites.

In those days, Mother had to be the organizer of the available foods for the family. Somewhere along the line, Mother, her sisters, and sisters-in-law decided that the acids in vinegar were the most important part of a diet. They made their vinegar from the apples that were brought in from Washington state, and had a contest for the best vinegar. It also seemed a priority to find as many uses for it as possible in every food we enjoyed.

Sauerkraut, sauerkraut, sauerkraut! It seems that cabbage grows almost everywhere in the world. When Mother's family came from Germany in 1878, they brought a traditional cabbage slicer with them. It was a box that slid back and forth on a board, with two forty-five degree steel blades for slicing cabbage to about a 1/16" thickness. The cabbage slicer made the rounds from family to family, to help fill a twenty-five gallon crockery jar with sauerkraut for each. The other vegetable that seems to grow anywhere is cucumbers, so consequently, we had pickles marinated in vinegar year around, too!

What do farm boys and girls do in the spring after being closed up in their homes all winter? They become restless and adventurous. For most kids, the spring was a time for horseback riding. It was a tradition that at noon on Sunday all the kids in a group from a fifteen-mile area would meet at the old, country Lutheran church yard. The fifty boys and girls would have races, competitions for the best saddles, bridles, red tars that went on the horse's bridle, and saddle blankets. A few of the more adventurous boys and girls brought their lariats. We would make a dummy, which was loose on the ground, and the kids would try to lasso the dummy. When they did, they would run off with it attached to their saddle.

We also had bareback riding contests. Like in the old cowboy movies, we would ride in such a way as to hide behind the side of the horse so the enemy could not shoot you. It was dangerous, but fun.

Sometimes the Indian kids would show up with their horses. Their spotted ponies were often smaller and skinnier than ours from living outdoors all winter.

Father and Mother helped us learn about the outside world by requiring Ray, Adeline, and I to read one "good book" a year. A "good book" was what we now consider a classic like *Wuthering Heights*, *Oil for the Lamps of China*, or *Tracks End*. My first choice was *Wuthering Heights*, which surprisingly became a great influence on my life.

I later became interested in history and concentrated on the Romanoff Empire. I am sure that I read at least a dozen books on Russian life from the 1600s to 1917 when Nicholas and Alexandra, together with their children, were murdered.

Our line to more exotic parts of the world came from our subscription to *National Geographic* magazine. In the twenties and thirties, each issue always carried a picture of some native who was "topless," a great attraction to us boys in the eight to twelve-year-old range.

Most people of my vintage can remember their first sight of a plane. One summer day when I was ten years of age, we were in our yard when we heard the roar of motors overhead. We could see these slow-flying planes, three of them, coming toward us very low.

We watched for the fly over, and resolved they were going west. We guessed that they were part of our army and been used in World War I. As the planes flew over us, I remember Mother running into the house and telephoning her sister, six miles to the west, and another relative about twelve miles further away, to alert them to the "big geese" that were coming toward them in the sky.

I also remember the countryside being alive with interest when a big "Blue Goose" landed in a pasture near our farm. By the time Father motored Mother and us three kids to see, we found that there were also hundreds of other people there.

The "Blue Goose" was a three-motor unit, which I believe was one of the first mail and passenger airplanes to be used in the country. We could see the corrugated tin that shaped its body, and the center propeller somewhat higher off the ground than the two side motors. It did not seem to be very well protected, because experimental boys like me had eased up the side of the plane and were writing our names on the tin. After that, I often wondered where my name flew during the life of that "Blue Goose."

Sometime in the late 1920s, our federal government passed a law eliminating the commercial brewing of beer and most all other alcoholic beverages. People who had never enjoyed drinking alcoholic beverages joined the "drinker" in challenging this new law.

In my home state of North Dakota, beer making became the hobby of the day. I had many relatives who joined in the foray, even though most had never frequented a bar before.

Father joined the pack and made us a beer-making family. Our family recipe was:

> 3-1/2 lb. plain dark malt syrup
> 3 cups brewing sugar
> 1 heaping teaspoon water crystals
> 1 oz. hop pellets
> 1 packet top fermenting yeast

> Dissolve the malt and brewing sugar in 3 quarts water, mix, add the water crystals and hop pellets.

> Boil for 10 minutes, add 3 gallons cold water in a brewing tub or crock. Add yeast and let ferment for seven days and bottle. Usually Father increased the proportions about six times to fill a 25 gallon crock.

> Let the beer set in the bottles for 3 - 4 weeks before cooling them for drinking.

Although we had electricity, we did not have refrigeration. So we would tie each bottle on a string and drop it into a well, twenty to twenty-five feet deep, which was the cool water level in our area. When the cap was popped, the farmers in North Dakota enjoyed the foamiest beer in the world.

It all came to an end in 1933 when the federal government gave up and repealed Prohibition. Father, like many other ranchers and farmers, never drank again.

All through the '20s, the economy of the country, and particularly in the agriculture and livestock area, was exceedingly good. My family had enjoyed living on top of the world . . . at least until the fall of 1929.

For years, we fed our hogs corn on the cob, with them only eating the kernels. Every day it fell on Ray, Adeline, and myself to go through the hog feeding area to pick up the old cobs. They made excellent heat in the stoves in our house, even though they burned fast and made feeding the fire a constant occupation.

At the time of land grants, there were also settlements under what the government called a "Tree Claim." If a person planted a certain number of trees on a quarter section of land, 160 acres, this piece of land became theirs. Father's family had three such tree claims. Since several of his siblings moved out of the area, this area was not cleared for thirty to forty years. Accordingly, Father had an idea to find fuel for our home from the dead or gnawed trees and broken limbs. He instructed Ray and I to take a team of horses, axes, and saws to bring home the wood. We had two sawhorses to lay the small trees or branches on for sawing, while Father wielded the ax.

During the Depression, thousands of farmers lost their land to banks, insurance companies, and shyster financiers. Father and Mother, as well as their families, agreed that they would never give up a single acre of land. In order to do this, we lived a very frugal life.

One way the families worked together was by assigning special duties to each household. My uncle and his wife ground wheat for our flour and cereal. The flour was edible, but the hot breakfast cereal was abominable. So, we were forced to turn homemade bread into our daily breakfast diet.

To keep this promise, Father and Mother also found ways to cut luxuries out of our lives, which wasn't very popular with the younger people. For example, moving pictures were just coming into being. Our little town hosted a motion picture every Friday evening. The people who supplied the picture went from town to town, with each having their regular night and time. Adult admission was twenty-five cents and children's was a dime. This made our family expense eighty cents per movie. Unfortunately, this was also the amount needed to save each week in order to pay the taxes on our land.

The movies had become a great source of entertainment for me. The first movie actress I fell in love with, at thirteen years of age, was Janet Gaynor. She was the greatest thing that ever hit the world, and I hoped to grow up and share my life with someone as beautiful. My second movie love was Jean Harlow. I remember Jean leading me from silent films to the talkies. I was, of course, disappointed when I had to give up my weekend entertainment. But "pin-ups" of the movie stars in my bedroom helped.

Daily, Father and Mother would talk of how to save money. Father had two ten-gauge, double-barrelled shotguns which he used for occasional hunting of wild geese and ducks. The geese would stop on their way south in the grain fields and cattle pastures to eat. At thirteen, Father took me hunting for the first time. He handed me one of the loaded guns and instructed me on how to enter the pasture. Father told me that I was to aim over my right shoulder to avoid hitting him. We walked along steadily without the geese noticing us, then suddenly, they took flight, and Father yelled "shoot." Two geese fell. I dropped the gun in the tall grass and took off after one goose that was only wounded. That was my big mistake.

After we collected our fallen geese, Father asked, "Okay, where is the gun?" Untethered prairie grass can be nearly three feet tall. A gun lying on the ground is visible only when you step on it. We looked for what seemed like hours, with Father getting angrier with every step . . . until we found it.

Gophers are another story. There were millions of gophers in the area and one summer our county government awarded a bounty of one cent for every gopher tail presented. Naturally, this was a young person's sport. Ray and I each had a small twenty-two rifle. There were bullets that were called "short" and "long." The short bullets cost one cent apiece and the long were one-and-a-half cents each. Nobody used the long bullets for obvious reasons - you would lose money.

The gophers would dig a hole in the ground, which was usually straight down. Then they would stick their heads up to see if it was safe to emerge. All the kids had their system of snaring the gopher. My idea was to make a loop of string about three inches in diameter, place it around the hole, then extend the string thirty to forty feet and lay still on the ground until the gopher emerged. When his head and shoulders popped up, I would jerk the string, and more times than not, snare my prey.

That year I delivered nearly 1,000 gopher tails.

Our land bordered the Northern Pacific Railroad's route from Chicago,

Minneapolis, and Fargo on to the West Coast. The passenger trains going both ways were usually loaded with travelers.

At certain times of the year, there were four passenger trains going in each direction. The farmers adjacent to the track relied on the train schedule for their breakfast, lunch, and dinner signals. The track was a single line, with a switch every hundred miles. If a train was late, a collision was imminent.

Farmers also relied on the trains' signals. The engineer's whistle communicated this basic message: Long, long, short, long...Here comes the train!

The Morse code was the railroad's telegraph system that consisted of a different signal for each of the twenty-six letters in the alphabet and the ten numbers of the numbering system. It was a long and tedious job to relay a message via Morse code because you had to spell out every letter of the word and every digit of the number.

Every kid was conscious of the telegraph system and had his copy of the codes. This is how we sent messages on the track with our hammers.

✯

Growing Up –
High School and Beyond

OUR TEACHERS WERE MR. DON BARR — THE SUPERINTENDENT, BAND leader, chemistry teacher, basketball coach of the junior teams, and Ms. Volberg Oslund, a beautiful, tall Norwegian woman of twenty-five years of age, who was the English, penmanship, home economics, and special activities teacher. Ms. Oslund also sponsored a series of one act plays for the high-school students to act in.

Somewhere along the line I read an article about "News Writing." In this article, they mentioned that the news story should answer all the "W" questions: Who? What? Where? When? and Why? I convinced Miss Oslund to teach a class on news writing. Our book was blue, with about 200 pages. We were assigned a story each week, which made this class more interesting than the others because we were able to directly apply our homework to everyday life.

Miss Oslund also taught a home economics class, with sewing as its main focus. Cloth was a treasured and expensive item, so one hundred pound flour sacks were used in class. Adeline, my sister, who was a terrific seamstress, made me three of the best pairs of boxer shorts. To everyone's delight, except mine, one pair had the sack company's name, "Occidental," along the front and the other two had it on the back.

"Marshall's Shorts," as they had been called, won first prize in the school sew-off. Then the teacher sent them to the county fair, where they also won first prize. Soon after, me and my blue-ribbon shorts became the hit of the high school. The goal of the high school girls was to see me wearing my shorts. I don't think any girl succeeded.

The third teacher, Mr. Ray Holst, was the basketball coach who pushed me further in the basketball field. Surprisingly, at about six foot and two inches, I was a tall fellow in the basketball field at the time. Every Friday we would have a game with one of the teams in our community, either at home or away.

My basketball career at the high school level was an enjoyable one, and our little team from Sanborn went on to the state tournament, ending with fourth place in our division. We only had a six-man team, which was typical for a small, rural community. So, we would take along a few girls to use as substitutes, if necessary. I cannot remember our team ever having to use one of the girls.

Sometimes people wonder what the turning point in their lives was, or will be. As I remember back, I recall a time Father and Mother took me to Valley City where there was a Jewish tailor. Much of his work had been done in the western theme of cowboy pants, shirts, bandannas, and rain jackets. Mother and Father enlisted him to make a suit for my high school graduation. The tailor was happy to have a chance to try his trade on a dress suit for a young man. He measured me from head to toe, and all the while I stood with the biggest smile on my face. A few weeks later, I attended my graduation with the most beautiful three-piece, gray suit in Sanborn.

Somewhere in the early grade school, Father and Mother decided that I should become a musical person. From the Sears catalog they bought me a violin with instructions on how to play simple tunes. I can remember being pretty good!

My favorite tune that I played, with Adeline singing, was: "I can play my violin just as good as Willie cin." I wore this tune out so much that the family soon gave up on any thought of my becoming a violinist, and instead bought me a trombone. In the seventh grade I was tooling away on the trombone and was accepted into the high school band. This isn't as grand a feat as it sounds. There were so few musical people in the area, no one else knew how to play the trombone. So, I was enlisted to be the first trombone player in Sanborn.

A traveling music teacher would come into the community and pick up eight to ten kids and take us to the school gym for "band practice." I wasn't very good, but I made a lot of noise. I participated through high school and my first two years of college, where I was the sixth (and last) trombone in the group. Thankfully, I was never called on to play solos.

At about twelve years of age it was decided that the time had come for me to learn to work as a farmer. It was Father's idea that I should follow him, and was given the responsibility of driving horses on every piece of machinery. I started by cultivating the corn in the middle of June, with the two slowest and quietest horses on the farm. They were a pretty good-looking pair of brown horses, about the same size, but the slowest animals that ever walked.

That same summer, I graduated from cultivating corn to making hay. I drove two horses on a mower with a five-foot sickle. Every noon and evening, having to take the sickle out of the mower while the horses ate, I gulped my lunch from the tin can and set off to sharpen the blade. About a week after the hay was cut, it was raked into winrows and then picked up with a buck rake and hauled into a hay stack to dry.

Because we had a large farm, much of the hay that we mowed ended up being put on a hayrack with pitchforks, then hauled with slings up into the top of the barn. Then a team would pull the hay to its destination. Once a sling was tripped, the hay fell down into what was called the haymow. For a few years, the cultivating and haying was my chief summer occupation.

At about thirteen years of age, I moved into driving four horses on a grain binder. We usually had about six binders going around the field. Soon, to Father's excitement, I was moved up from sixth to fourth place in the binder parade.

A binder was a rather intricate machine in the late twenties, and because I understood the mechanics of its operations, I found myself one of the lead repairmen in fixing any problems. This, too, gave me a feeling of importance.

Thrashing was always a big fall event that I usually watched from the sidelines. Our farm community would start in the south and work north with a thrashing crew. I had a neighbor boy who was about my age, but half my size, who joined the crew with me. Our fathers decided that the two of us, at fourteen years of age, should be equal to one man. To keep everything in balance, I was given one horse from my farm and little Nels was given one horse from his farm, Father supplied the wheels and wagon and Nels' father supplied the hay rack.

We started out on the twentieth of August and worked our way north. There were about twenty men in the crew, plus Nels and me. For food we had a cook wagon, which was similar to the old wagons of the west. However, we had one advantage - our cooks were two girls from the farm community. It didn't take me long to decide which would be mine. But, I never succeeded in stamping my territory. They liked the older fellows better than me.

Every night we slept in a barn. Father and Mother always warned us of the danger of barn fires from thrashing crews, as liquor was always prominent and there were always a few that were heavy users. Back then, everyone "rolled their own cigarettes" and, of course, Nels and I were led into trying tobacco for the first time. In previous years, I had experimented like most farm kids when I would smoke dried leaves rolled in newspaper. When I tried the real cigarettes I got sick, which became my deterrent from smoking until this day.

Because of the fire danger, Nels and I always made our bed in the hay closest to the doors. Our schools usually started about the fifteenth of September, when the work was supposed to be done. Since Nels and I were making about a dollar and a quarter a day, we were not ready to go back to school. In fact, we kept moving north until about the first of October, when we headed our team of horses and our hayrack to the south and returned to our homes.

When I returned to school, I decided that the world was not moving fast enough for me. So, I decided to take a load-and-a-half of school work to finish high school in three years. This would allow me to graduate at age sixteen.

Normally we associate leadership with fast-moving, intelligent, educated men and women. We can't go wrong using that as a basis for accomplishing things in the world.

However, in the animal kingdom, there are leaders who are just as determined to accomplish things and succeed in their lives. This includes horses.

Horses were the main power of the farming industry. Successful farmers had to use the same strategy that tractor farms do today. Father was considered one of the outstanding farmers in the area.

In farming, there are two-horse, three-horse, four-horse, six-horse, and eight-horse teams. On our farm, the six-horse team was determined to be the most efficient. One man could handle that size unit where the horses were lined up in two formations - three and three for plows and narrow machinery, six abreast for wider machinery. Horses could work farmland within a three-mile radius of their housing. Like people, they can only work about five hours before needing food and drink. Then the team can go back for another five to six hours of work. Traveling back and forth to a barn wastes time. So, instead we had two barns six miles apart, each with twelve horses.

In the first barn, Father had a big, black Percheron with a white blaze down his face and four white, long-haired anklets, similar to the Budweiser horses. His name was Prince, and he was a true leader. When he was in a team of six abreast, he was always the third horse from the right, looking at them from the driver's seat. He walked fast and was guided by the lines with the slightest pull on the reins. He was not happy unless he was a nose length ahead of the other five horses in the team. When it came to turning around, he was always the leader, and most of the time he made the corners with a little trot.

When the team is spread out, as they call stagecoach power units, Prince was always the lead horse and on the right of the three-horse team. I can remember with great satisfaction the leadership that Prince exercised over his team.

On the other farm we also had a leader, Jack, who was a big mule. It was unusual for mules to be living in North Dakota. We associated mules with the south, not the frigid climate of the north. I so admired that mule, and was taken with his differences in appearance, that Uncle Ferd gave him to me. Father found a place for Jack in the second barn, where he held the leader position in many of the teams.

When we would break the new colts to harness, they were teamed up with Prince or Jack to learn to drive, pull, and work in two-horse teams.

A farm horse in our area lived to be about twenty years old. At three years, they were broken to the harness and would become a working horse. Horses older than twenty had a difficult time living through the cold winters of North Dakota. At fifteen years of age, Father rotated the horses, so the older ones would be in the number-two barn.

In the spring, preparing twenty-four harnesses for field work was a big job for the hired men. Usually we had four workers, and led by Father, they worked the farm. It was not uncommon to have six, four-horse teams, with each pulling a binder with drivers. As a thirteen-year-old farm boy, driving one of the binders made me feel like I was on top of the world. There was no greater joy than commanding four horses pulling a binder, with a lot of wheels turning. I loved watching the golden stalks slide up the rolling canvas and into the mechanism that produced a bundle. The bundle carrier accommodated approximately ten bundles, and when full, the driver would trip a lever to unload them.

One of the most interesting occupations for a farm boy was driving the farm plow. My team was three-and-three strung out, and I wanted either Prince or Jack as my lead. As I rode the plow, I could see the furrows turn over and reveal the black dirt of North Dakota.

I drove the gang plow, which really only had two lathes, and so I don't know how it got the name "gang." It could be pulled by four, five or six horses. Depending on the size of the team, the gang plow could cover as little as ten, and as many as fourteen miles a day

As the furrows turned over, they would expose worms that the seagulls would go after. It seemed strange to have seagulls in North Dakota, since it is about as far as you can get from the sea in any direction. From my understanding, seagulls can appear almost anywhere. So, in all the thinking time that I would have sitting on the plow, I would wonder if the seagull should really be called the "world gull."

During my teen years, I was continually reminded by my parents and other relatives that the oldest son was expected to take over the farm and be experienced in all the duties involved.

Helping pass on older horses was a lesson I learned when I was fifteen. Father came to me and said, "Today is the day we take care of Dick and Punch." They were a team of white horses who had passed their prime. Father and I took old Dick out behind the barn. Father shot him with a rifle, between the eyes. He fell to the ground, and after some time Father handed me a skinning knife. We took the skin off old Dick on one side, then with the help of other horses, turned him over and took off the other side. To do this, Father put a chain around his ankle at the front leg and another at the back. Then we hooked the chains to a heavy log about eight feet long and hitched it to the horse. The horse pulled and old Dick flipped over.

Then he brought out old Punch and handed me the rifle. After giving me a little story of how it was necessary for the oldest boy in every family to know how to handle all the experiences of farm life, he guided the rifle and pointed to the spot where I should aim. For days after, I could not help but feel that I had committed a terrible sin against one of my friends, old Punch.

Horse hides at the time were worth a lot of money. The hides had to be preserved by smearing rock salt on the skinned side. The hides were folded into a sixteen-inch square, then left outside to freeze.

To dispose of the carcasses, we took another team of horses, and fastened the chains around the ankles and hauled them into an area about a half mile from the barn. We would try to find an incline to hide the carcasses from site, but often, because there are not hills in North Dakota, they would be left to rot wherever we had an open space.

Wolves would often try to eat the carcasses. We would carefully set traps to stop them. Wolves are sensitive to the human scent, so we would cover the traps with straw, and to eliminate the human odors, we would burn the straw.

I remember shortly after Punch and Dick's deaths, we caught a wolf! What an exciting feeling for a young boy.

Machinery and cars were always a part of my life, from the early days on.

In the Sears catalog of 1930 there was an attachment for a Ford Model T tractor conversion kit. We took the wheels off the rear of the Ford car, and put on the large steel wheels, probably forty-eight inches in diameter, with steel lugs about three inches long to dig into the soil.

The motor of the Ford, running at medium speed, was able to pull the equivalent of a four-horse team. The problem was that this Ford motor did not have an automatic starter. We had to crank the motor to get it running. It was difficult to turn the crank. Once I sprained my back and was unable to work for several weeks. But Ray and I thought this tractor was the heyday of the world and we had it running as much as possible.

At some point, Father found two Saxon cars. These were single, three-person seaters with very small motors. These two convertibles made Ray and I the outstanding young men of the community. We were never without girls to ride with, and since our area was sparsely settled, it was not hard to find a spot to be romantic. There were days when Mother worried about me and the girls. I am sure that many a night Father and Mother waited up late for us to come home from some of our good times with the Saxons.

We enjoyed these two Saxons for four summers, from 1930 until 1933. Soon after, I left home to attend the University of Minnesota.

Ray has never been one to enjoy all the history of our family, the antiques that accumulated, and items that have reached their full age. I am sure that somewhere along the line after he came back from the University of Minnesota, these same Saxons ended up in the scrap heap. However, since World War II was on the brink in 1941, I doubt that either of these treasures ended up in the Japanese war machine. But I do think they were two of the greatest assets that any two young boys could have enjoyed.

Two of my cousins, a teacher in Cody, Wyoming and his brother, were home on a summer visit when they invited me to attend the World's Fair with them. Mother and Father made a fuss about me going so far away because they still saw me as their little boy. But, after a lot of pleading, they agreed to let me go and would give me just enough money for food and lodging for our two-week stay.

The roads were all two lane and made of gravel. It took us three long days to make the 700 mile trip. Once in Chicago, we found a small hotel on Madison Avenue, about five miles west of the downtown area where the World's Fair was being held.

One morning, we were approached by a lady reporter and a photographer from the Chicago Tribune. Visitors from as far away as North Dakota were uncommon, so she took advantage of our naiveté and printed our picture in the paper the next day.

In return, I took advantage of talking business with this reporter on a topic that I remembered from my news writing class. Before we left, she had given me a pencil and paper and told me to write a story as if I was still in the class. My story was printed in the paper, and as you can imagine, the story of a seventeen-year-old boy with his story and photograph in a Chicago paper was unbelievable. We bought several copies and mailed them back to North Dakota where my mother showed them to half the people in the state.

There is another memorable incident from this trip. The Chrysler Corporation had a large exhibit of a punch press, which was fed a strip of three-inch-wide aluminum, which went in one end while ashtrays dropped out the other. This fascinated me. And to think that in later years I would operate a press which could punch out 240,000 corners for aluminum windows in eight hours.

Our community was infatuated with me and my new worldly experience. No one else had gone to the Fair or had been so far away. Every time someone new saw me, I was besieged with questions of what I had learned, seen, and experienced

In the depth of the Depression and the height of the droughts in our area, I was finishing my two-year study at the State Teachers College in Valley City. Nobody was getting a job because of the economic conditions, and anyone who had one held on to it for dear life.

In the middle of the summer when I had finished cultivating, Don Barr, the Superintendent of my high school at the time, wrote me from a town sixty miles west of Sanborn, where he was now the Superintendent.. I had not been in communication with him since leaving high school, and had not known where he was now living. Surprisingly, he told me he had a vacancy in his school and offered me the position. He had seen my name as an honor recipient of the teachers college and always believed I would be a grand teacher.

Since our only communication was by letter, Mother was very interested in getting my job acceptance to Mr. Barr. She found a neighbor lady, whose husband was Hail Commissioner for the state, to take us to Medina. Mr. Barr arranged a room for me and a place to take my meals. At nineteen years of age, I made seventy-five dollars a month teaching the seventh and eighth grades.

By coincidence, this was the same size school I had attended. Four teacher in the lower grades, and three for high school. I was determined to be a great success, and prepared my teaching plans in advance and always tried to make learning an enjoyable time for the students. Humor was a good part of my strategy, but laced with facts and innovative ideas. The parents in the community soon decided that I was a "pretty good guy," even though I was nineteen and showed an interest in several of the older girls.

Medina basketball became my passion because of my own years of playing. There were seven young men who were interested in playing and whose parents would let them participate. Some families, especially those of Russian descent, did not value athletics as my family had. Therefore, not all of the male students participated.

Our basketball season was a great success. We were the champions from our division of twenty-five schools, which came from a large, sparsely-settled county in central North Dakota. There was great excitement and surprise that the Medina team had gotten so far, and I received a dinner invitation from the family of each player. We won at districts and went on to the regionals, where we were finally defeated.

That summer, on the night of July 19th, our family went to bed poor, but happy. At about 4:00 A.M. there was an explosion of lightning, and our biggest barn, my parents' pride and joy, exploded and burned to the ground. Normally there would have been twelve horses and fifty head of cattle in the barn. However, since it was summer, there were only five horses, a horned thoroughbred bull, and about half a dozen calves. Naturally, we lost them all. It was a tremendous loss, not just in value, but also in the love that we had for these animals.

During fires, horses tend to run into a barn instead of away from it. I can still see Father running down to shut the gate so the other horses could not go into the fire. The barn burned for two hours before all the walls caved in. In one corner, there were a thousand bushels of oats in a bin on the second floor, directly over the horses. They fell down on top of the horses, who, hopefully, were dead by this time. Grains burn very slowly, and it smoldered for at least two months.

Since it was the middle of the summer, Father built a feeding rack about fifty foot long, where hay was placed in the center and oats in the troughs on each side. We had to round up five more horses from our friends, the Sioux Indians. It was only a matter of days until Father had twelve horses, six on each side of this outdoor feeding rack. One of my uncles contributed "Lottie," who was a big, white horse, and another contributed a dapple brown named "Topsy."

Horses have a tendency to fight when they are able to get at each other. Since we could not afford stalls, I was awakened at night by tremendous horse fights that Father, Ray, and I had to stop. These fights never seemed to end, and to predetermine which two horses were going to fight was never possible.

Luckily, the barn that burned was insured. The only problem was getting the money out of the insurance company. Father argued furiously with the adjuster until his claim was paid. This became my first lesson in being a firm, steadfast negotiator.

We chose another area for the new barn and hired Frank Hesch, a sturdy German contractor, to build it before the cold weather set in. Every weekend I hitchhiked twelve miles home from school to help Father make new stanchions to hold the cows' heads in place.

Normally, I would have been expected to stay at home and work the farm, as I was the oldest son. However, in addition to the Depression, which was still stretched out for the sixth year, we also had a severe drought in the western states. We had the drought, wind, cacti, and piles of dust. We lived with wet towels under the doors and window sills to keep the dirt away from our faces. With these conditions, Father and Mother decided that farming was going to be a thing of the past. They encouraged me instead to further my education at the University of North Dakota.

The University was about seventy miles east and seventy miles north of Sanborn. To save money, I hitchhiked. When I arrived in Grand Forks, I knew I had to get a job in order to survive. Somehow, I found out that the Lambda Chi Fraternity house needed a caretaker for the summer. I took the job, which also gave me a place to sleep until the new school year began, when I would go back to my second year of teaching. One day I went to downtown Grand Forks and was given a job clearing tables at the local hotel. I soon worked my way up to being a waiter. In addition to the University, Grand Forks was a center of economic progress in the northeast corner of North Dakota. Quite a few people came to the hotel from out of the state, and I was always interested in talking with them about the lifestyles in other parts of the country.

I signed up for three classes — history, English, and Chaucer. The Chaucer class was carried on in Old English. It was hard enough speaking reasonably good English, but in this class, we were to decipher and speak in what seemed to be a foreign language.

At the Lambda Chi house, there were three young men who were medical students at the University of Minnesota who had come to Grand Forks for summer school. We became friendly and spent a great deal of time together. Realizing my poor background, they suggested a new field of study — Certified Public Accounting.

I have realized over the many years since that summer that my life's work really came from a passing acquaintance with these three young men.

After my summer at the University of North Dakota, I returned to my seventh and eighth grade students for a wonderful year of teaching. In June, basking in the knowledge from the previous summer, I decided to try my luck at the University of Minnesota. I grabbed the money I saved from my teaching salary, and headed off for Minneapolis on a railroad ticket that cost me twelve dollars and sixty-two cents.

With my meager bank account, I knew I had to find a job to supplement my school work. I registered for three classes — economics, business law, and beginning accounting. I bought books, paper, pencils, and saw my bank account dwindle. The University had an employment office to assist students who needed financial help. It always helps to make things run smoothly when you befriend someone who may help you. I met a young lady in the office, and after visiting her for several days, she gave me a contact. She said there was a company that made Zwieback toast, and that I should talk with Mr. Dalzell.

The bakery marketed their products on a house-to-house basis with horse-drawn wagons. Mr. Dalzell was fascinated with the fact that I had come from a farm and was able to talk "horse sense" with him. He walked me through the barns where I felt right at home with the odors I had grown up with. I thought Mr. Dalzell was going to give me a job running the stable, which was the last thing I wanted.

On the second interview, he offered me the position of assistant cashier. My hours were from four until ten P.M., six days a week. He paid me twelve dollars a week, or two dollars a day. The University and the bakery were five miles apart, and it cost me ten cents each way to ride the street car. Since Mr. Dalzell knew I was working my way through school, he allowed me to take home two items of unsold bread, rolls, cookies, and pie every day. This quickly became my entire food source.

After living for some time in the YMCA, I found a young fellow, who also grew up in North Dakota, to share an apartment. A few weeks after I moved in, we ran across an old friend of mine from Sanborn. Ed Burton moved in with us, and the three of us shared this apartment for two years.

Ed also added to my weekly food budget from the bakery. He supplied dried prunes and apricots, which I learned to make into a great sandwich. You simply take a prune, open it, remove the pit, and put several between two slices of bread. This quickly became the mainstay of my lunches for two years.

Life at the University was uneventful. Early rise, walk to class, study, and off to work. There was little time for any extracurricular activities. I hated the fact that I didn't have time to become friendly with some of the beautiful girls that I met.

In June, 1938 I graduated from the University of Minnesota. Father and Mother came to see the first member of their family to graduate from a four-year university. We had some distant relatives who lived nearby and allowed Father and Mother to stay with them. They were kindly folk and chauffeured and fed my family for four days.

The big question after graduation was to decide what to do with the knowledge that earned you a degree. I remembered back to the medical student friends I met many years before. They had suggested the Certified Public Accountant field. I was primed for this new business venture and ready to take on the big accounting firms.

F o u r

★

The Beginning of
My Business Career

ONE OF THE BIG EIGHT ACCOUNTING FIRMS IN NEW YORK CITY HIRED ME for their Wall Street Office. I set off hitchhiking with only nine dollars in my pocket and four days to get there.

In Madison, Wisconsin, I met a young, seemingly wealthy girl, who was a student at the University of Wisconsin and owned her own car. I can't imagine why, but she picked me up and offered to drive me to Cleveland, Ohio. I decided I must have looked harmless.

Whenever we stopped for something to eat, she always insisted on paying. When we came near to Chicago she said she was going to have to stay in a hotel overnight because her father and mother had given her strict instructions. I didn't know what to say or do. I thought "I have to handle this with kid gloves." I asked if she minded if I slept in the car. She never offered to have me go into the hotel. Since I was still six hundred miles from my destination, with three hundred potential miles with her, I decided to sleep in the car and not give in to my urge.

She also told me she had a very good friend in New York City, and suggested I communicate with her when I arrived. Some months later, when I had enough money to buy a new shirt, tie, and underwear, I called her. She was a nice young lady who lived with her mother in an apartment in Yonkers. When they heard I was living at the YMCA and eating all my meals at fruit stands and automats, they felt sorry for me offered to let me move into their extra bedroom. What an offer! But I decided that I would be "making my bed" and would end up with a situation that I could not get out of. I knew I had to work for several years to pass my C.P.A. and get some experience before the money started rolling in.

When I arrived in New York City to start my job, I had two dollars and twenty-five cents to my name. I think that if I had asked the manager of the firm, he might have given me an advance. But I decided that would be the wrong thing to do, although I was paying a quarter each night, cash in advance, to sleep at the YMCA. That totaled three-and-a-half dollars for a two-week stay, which didn't leave any money to buy food.

I might never had made it the two weeks, except that my years of athletics while growing up ended up saving the day. The accounting firm had a softball team that played three nights a week out on Jefferson Beach. While playing second base for the team, I also made some very good friends. One of them, Miss Best, had a father who owned the Best Pencil Company. These were the same pencils that I had used as a kid and college student.

When she heard that I left Minnesota with nine dollars and arrived without enough money to sleep and eat on, she offered me ten dollars a week until I got paid. By staying at the YMCA and eating a roll and drinking juice for breakfast, I managed to eat and sleep those first two weeks on less than twenty-three dollars. I scraped up five bucks out of each of my two-weeks pay until I was out of debt.

Every young accountant aspires to become a Certified Public Accountant. In 1938 and 1939, the profession was new and I got a lucky break from a friend who provided a job that would advance my career.

Robert Trueblood, a friend from North Dakota and a fellow accountant, told me that a professor at Northwestern University was looking for proofreading help on an accounting textbook. We approached our employers about this idea, and because summer is a slow time for our profession, we were given ninety days to complete this task in Chicago.

This textbook represented the materials required for the C.P.A. exam. We were fortunate to have dozens of problems solved and explained to us in this book. After applying to the State of Illinois for the C.P.A. exam, we began proofreading enthusiastically.

The C.P.A. exam is given over two days, and I felt that as the youngest person in the room, I was also the most nervous. Two questions were particularly troubling. The first was on the pricing of the body of a pig - how much for the pork chops, bacon, pork hocks, and spareribs. I spent hours on this and thought I was being hit with a question I was unprepared to answer.

The second question was how to price a lawn mower, assuming that your company bought fifty percent of the parts and manufactured fifty percent. We were given many factors related to pricing, including overhead, labor, sales costs, marketing costs, and advertising.

In January, the results were out and I had passed the exam! Shortly after, I applied to the American Institute of Accountants and received the 732nd certificate of membership. Accountants who had been working in the industry for years were just realizing the benefits and opportunities of joining a professional organization.

About thirty days later, the organization welcomed its new C.P.A. members with a dinner. Twenty-five of us were introduced that night. The Master of Ceremonies commented when he announced me that I was the youngest C.P.A. in Illinois. I was just twenty-three.

If I took assignments out of New York City, my food and lodging expenses were paid as part of the trip. The next thing I knew, I was in Des Moines, Iowa, working for a large food company that was developing a line of frozen products. This company had a lot of people picking strawberries and planned to freeze the berries within a couple hours of their leaving the vine. Now, this seems like a normal process, but

The Early Years

LEO ERNST NOECKER
1-7-1836 to 3-1-1917
b. Westphalia, Germany
CANADA*1857   DAKOTA TERRITORY*1879

This is an early photograph of your grandfather, Leo Noecker. To you he may be great, or great great ancestor. Photography was in its infancy in the 1890's when this picture was taken and therefore it is an antique for this reason also. In the early days in Dakota Territory, farmers and ranchers went buffalo hunting in the same manner as men in today's times go duck, geese, pheasant, or deer hunting, except in the olden days, men went on horseback. On one of these forays, Leo shot two buffalo, skinned them, and tanned the hides. From these two hides he made this coat with his own hands. Tailors weren't available in those days. The story goes that he wore this coat for thirty winters until his death in 1917. Note that he's a pretty sharp DUDE — a muffler around his neck — a gold watch chain with a gold fob. You could do well to emulate his success.

William Noecker (my father) courting Pauline Brock, motivated by Dolly, the horse. (1910) The buggy, now eighty-eight years old is in Florida with our daughter, Nancy.

Top left: Maternal grandparents Gustav and Amelia Brock settled in Dakota Territory in 1878.

Top right: Uncle Leo Noecker (1910).

Left: Marshall and Adeline Noecker, their first home in North Dakota.

Below: Grandfather Leo Noecker standing in field. From the left is the barn, the granary, the machine shed, and the home. Marshall was born here in 1915.

Marshall and Adeline in the barnyard.
(1917)

Bringing in the sheaves.

My father, William
Noecker, moving his
thrashing equipment from
one farm to another.

Birdseye view of the north side of Sanborn, North Dakota. All of the larger buildings
on the left side of Main Street were destroyed by a fire in 1919.

William Noecker's second traveling thrashing machine was in full operation by 1900.

Two female cooks and the cooking shack in the background
traveled from farm to farm with William Noecker's thrashing crew. (1910)

A Noecker-Knight steam thrashing machine in full operation. (1915)

Top: A bird's eye view of Sanborn, North Dakota as it stands today.

Center: Marshall at the crank of one of two identical Saxon roadsters purchased by Marshall's father for his two sons. The roadsters made us very popular boys. (1932)

Lower right: Eighth grade graduation.

Modern farming in North Dakota. The Erna and Lloyd Anderson family. (1997)

Left: Marshall Noecker, president of Kaufmann Corp., looks out for the future of his company and community.

Right: Chest of drawers made by Marshall in 1942, when he was trying to determine what his life's work should be. He also made a baby bed, single bed, dining room table, and two end tables.

The inventory as shipped from Kaufmann Corporation in Detroit to the franchises.

The fabricating area for making the windows and the doors.

A group of windows in the New Castle, England warehouse ready for shipment.

A group of doors ready for shipment from the New Castle, England franchise.

Right: Sandra and Marshall in Belgium visiting Wim Limericks, one of our European window manufacturers. (1972)

Below: Robert Smith, Marshall Noecker, David Padilla, and Robert Yazejian — the group responsible for what we think is the manufacture of more windows than any other company in the world.

Top: Noecker architectural project: an inside view of a tunnel connecting two Detroit high rise office buildings eleven stories above the street.

Below: An outside view of a tunnel similar to the one in the above photo.

Left: Sandra and Marshall on their first trip away from the family. LeEstrail, Quebec.

Bottom Left: Marshall and Sandra enjoying a side trip to Malaga, Spain. What a party!

Bottom Right: Enjoying the Ascot Horse Races in England (near London).

Top: Sandra and Marshall as guests of British royalty at Kensington Palace. A distinguished rider and horse.

Left: Inside the main gates of the Kremlin in Moscow, Russia. Four wonderful days of sightseeing.

Top: In the main dining room of the Michaela Rose, a 176-foot ocean-going yacht owned by Margaret and Trammell Crow. In the Baltic Sea, near St. Petersburg, Russia.

Bottom Left: Enjoying an eight-day trip on the Royal Caribbean (a gift from our eight children.

Bottom Right: In San Juan, Puerto Rico visiting the first window dealer manufacturer outside of the U.S.A.

Top: Sandra and Marshall in Beijing, China as guests of the Chinese government.

Left: Sandra in Brussels, Belgium with Belgium residents Alistar and Jesse Mitchell. The occasion was son Richard's musical group opening the 1996 European Jazz Festival.

Top: Long-time friend of the family, Helen Guo Lan-Xia, Government employee in Beijing, China.

Center: With son, Nicholas, in Edinburgh, Scotland. Visiting favorite window manufacturing franchises.

Bottom: Marshall and Sandra at a cowboy and Indian party they hosted at the Hunt Club, Grosse Pointe Farms.

In London for the wedding of Sophie Speller, daughter of the Right Honorable Anthony Speller and his wife, Maureen. From left: Marshall, daughter Alexandra, a friend of Nicholas, son Nicholas, and Sandra.

Tony Speller (left), member of the British parliament in first the Margaret Thatcher and then John Major governments. Since retiring from day to day politics he works world-wide as an Environmental Consultant specializing in helping clients make money from waste or 'left overs' from their work. This includes the organic recycling of household and domestic waste to produce composts, soil cover and purified water.
Main areas of operation are Europe, Australia, and New Zealand.
Mrs. Maureen Speller (right) is an Examiner for Trinity College, London, in Speech and Drama. She travels the world examining students of every age and advising teachers on standards and grades. Recent visits have included Italy, Ireland, and France. Later in the year a stay of eight weeks will cover New Zealand.

Daughter Nancy raises thoroughbred Dutch Warmbloods on her Florida ranch. Marshall, with horse number two (1993). The father of these colts lives in Holland.

back then it was a new idea. My job was to determine the costs of paying the strawberry growers and the frozen food trucks used to deliver the berries to stores, plus all other incidental costs. A few weeks later, I was back in Des Moines to determine the cost of taking sweet corn from the stock through freezing and packaging.

While on the road, a lot of interesting things happened. One night, for example, I was in a bar drinking beer with the young fellow who was working with me. We met a couple of girls who were probably a few years older than us. We talked, had a few beers, and laughed away the evening. The next night when we went to the State Fair, we ran across these ladies again. However, this time they were dragging along two ragamuffin kids and told us they were the wives of pig farmers who were showing their pride at the fair. They had enjoyed a night out on the town the previous evening.

A few weeks later, on another trip to Des Moines, we met two other young ladies who we enjoyed drinks and laughs with. Like before, they did not tell us they were married, but I found out a few days later while visiting a local dentist. Surprisingly, the receptionist was one of the ladies and the dentist's wife. No mention was made of our meeting, and I never went back to that dentist.

Another time I was working on an audit of the Schwinn Bicycle Company in Chicago. The Schwinn people gave me two tickets to attend a bicycle race. At that time, indoor bicycle races were common, particularly in Europe. The number of riders on this indoor track was amazing — more than thirty, with their bright colors designating the country they represented. The riders raced around the track, speeding like drivers at the Indy 500, with only inches between them.

The accounting profession was good to me. I enjoyed the experience and the opportunity to see how people were making money. But after three years of moving from small business to small business, I concluded that I was smarter than many of the owners who ran them.

In 1939 Hitler was moving around Europe in an unfriendly manner and there were some expectations that this would soon bring our country into the conflict. These expectations proved true and the country started to prepare for war.

Like many young men, on October 20, 1940, I registered for the draft. While not in the lower quartile, I was in the thirty percent bracket, which could have sent me to war within the year.

In July of 1941, my manager called me into his office to discuss how the company was concerned about the draft status of their young male employees. He suggested I take a job in the defense industry, which would make me essential to the war effort, but defer the draft. A new client in Benton Harbor, Michigan, who built small boats, needed help. The company had built many small boats during World War I, and later for the Chicago World's Fair. After that, their assets lay in abeyance for eight years until a Chicago promoter secured a government loan and planned to reopen the company. After meeting this promoter, I took the job and moved to Benton Harbor to assist in his ventures.

Benton Harbor was a quiet town for a single man - too quiet! I had to have a car, so I went shopping at the local Ford dealer. They only had a two-door coupe. Because Ford Motor Company was no longer making cars for civilian use, the salesman told me I had better take that car or be happy with a used one. I bought the last two-door Ford coupe for $838. What a joy to get wheels.

F i v e

⭐

Harriet

A YEAR EARLIER, I HAD ALREADY MET THE WOMAN WHO LATER BECAME my wife. In the fall of 1940, I went to Detroit with a friend, Al Clayboe, to do an audit for the Household Finance Corporation. While there, I called the Kaufmann family in Grosse Pointe on the advice of the grandmother, whom I had met in Chicago (and who also was from North Dakota, though a generation or two removed from me).

I was flabbergasted when Harriet's mother invited us to dinner, because Grosse Pointe was at the height of society and fashion in Michigan.

When I walked in the door I became immediately smitten with the young lady of the house. Her name was Harriet, and she was different than any other girl I had met before. When I came back to Detroit in January, I was again invited to dinner. This time, however, was not as happy. Harriet had an engagement ring on her finger, and when she drove me to the bus station, she confirmed my worst fear.

I was determined not to give up. I called her monthly, from February through August. During the last call, she told me she had broken off her engagement and I immediately invited her for a visit to Benton Harbor. She accepted. We danced at the country club and spent the weekend totally involved in one another. On Sunday, while driving to the train station, I started talking about getting married. Her response was, "I thought you would never ask."

On November 29, 1941 we were married at her home in Grosse Pointe. Our first home was a nice second-floor apartment on a hill overlooking Lake Michigan in Benton Harbor. We had two bedrooms and a very nice bathroom. The apartment building had four units, two upstairs and two down. The owner was Fred Upton, who was the founder of the Whirlpool washing machine and dryer factory. Mr. and Mrs. Upton were very nice and gave us a brand new Whirlpool washing machine. This became our prized possession because is was the first appliance we owned.

Work with the boat yard often took me to Washington, D.C. to collect money for the minesweepers and PT boats we were building. I would get into the city in the morning and leave in the evening with a check for as much as several hundred thousand dollars. Shortly after we were married, my employer, who was very pleased with my marriage and thought Harriet was a wonderful woman, told me to take her on my next trip. We left on a Thursday evening and took the overnight train to Washington, D.C. We stayed the weekend and saw the sights.

As I look back on our courtship I am amazed at how few times Harriet and I actually saw each other before the wedding. I would have to liken it to the horse-and-buggy days when hundreds of miles separated you from the one you loved. After our third meeting, the weekend that Harriet traveled to Benton Harbor to visit, until our wedding, I am sure that we didn't see each other more than three times. For a courtship limited to six meetings before the wedding, everything worked out. It was a very successful marriage.

★

Going into Business

IN 1941 I DECIDED I WANTED TO START MY OWN BUSINESS. I TEAMED UP with two other young fellows to buy a brass foundry for $2,990, of which I contributed $700. We had three employees, and our biggest customer was the ship-building company where I worked. Unfortunately, we realized the company could not survive with the high labor costs and small market niche.

So I turned my interest toward a more lucrative venture — furniture. The ship yard was filled with old mahogany planks and boards left over from World War I. The manager told me that this Philippine mahogany was the best in the world, but because of the war, Honduran was cheaper and easier to get.

I drew plans for end tables, four-drawer dressers, beds, dining-room tables, and baby beds. The end tables seemed the simplest, so I started there. I had built every piece up to the baby bed. Harriet, the more creative and artistic of the two of us, designed it. The bed required some mass production for its fifteen rails and thirty stays. When I finished the bed, at 11:00 P.M. on September 27, 1942, it was just hours before our first son, Chip (Marshall junior), was born. What timing!

On one of my many trips to Washington, D.C. to collect money from the Navy, I had the good fortune to meet Admiral Forrestal, whom I recognized from his picture in the papers. He was talking with some men as I stood nearby to listen. At the end of his conversation he turned and shook my hand, and we started talking. He asked my profession, and when I explained that it was Certified Public Accounting, his face lit up. He explained that he wanted me to join the Navy instead of working for a small shipyard building minesweepers. He thought that this war would be different — a war where C.P.A.s would be in great demand. He left with an invitation for me to call his office the next time I was in Washington.

On the train home to Benton Harbor, I tried to think of how to get into a Navy program. I decided to write to a dozen of the most prominent industrialists in the country and ask if I could serve their company's war effort. Harriet helped me compose a letter stating that I wanted to help them by taking over their minor duties. We sent copies to the presidents of General Electric, General Motors, and two prominent ship builders, among others.

I received seven replies, and two letters of interest. One was from Andrew Higgins, a ship builder from New Orleans, inviting me to visit at his expense. Harriet and I took the train from Chicago to New Orleans in the spring of 1943. Within a half hour of meeting Mr. Higgins, I was employed by Higgins Industries.

Then he asked how soon I could start. I was really sweating on how to handle this because my employer in Benton Harbor had been so nice, accommodating, and friendly to Harriet and me. Before our son was born, we had often watched his two children while he traveled with his wife on business. It turned out that I did not need to worry because my employer was supportive of my career advancement, and even gave us several hundred dollars as a going-away present.

We packed up and headed south. Unfortunately, one item that did not move with us was our prized washing machine. Just before we moved, it was stolen from our garage by two men who said they were picking it up for repairs. Our neighbor, who saw the whole thing and even questioned the men, believed their story and we never saw the washer again.

During the last hundred miles of driving to New Orleans through Bayou country, water lapped at the road on both sides, and huge weeping willow trees lined the way with vines hanging down into the water. These were sights we had never seen before, and from our little car, with a baby in the back, it was quite the experience. We pulled into a little motel called the Alamo Plaza on St. Charles Avenue. The next morning, I was up early to head to the plant to discuss with Mr. Higgins and the company treasurer, Mr. Gottesman, what my role with the company would be. They gave me a desk outside Mr. Gottesman's office in the City Park plant and told me to go home and rest for the next day.

Harriet thought I needed a new wardrobe for my job. We found a tailor who agreed to make three new suits for thirty-five dollars each. A few weeks later, when we picked them up, I felt like a king walking around in tailor-made suits. These were my first new suits since my parents bought me one for my high school graduation.

Harriet, Chip, and I lived in the motel for a few weeks, which was especially difficult for Harriet who had to manage a seven-month-old baby. There was no air conditioning in most homes or motels at that time, so it was terribly hot and uncomfortable. While I had always looked down on this practice, I soon joined the majority of men in the South who just wore an undershirt when at home — it was just too damn hot otherwise! The last thing I did before going to work was to slip on my dress shirt, and the last thing before getting out of my car at the office was to put on my tie.

Mr. Gottesman took pity on us and arranged for us to rent a small, two-bedroom house on De Saix Boulevard, near the City Park plant. While the house did not have air conditioning either, it did have cross ventilation. We took maximum advantage of this and installed a permanent fan in the kitchen window and a removable fan in the bedroom window. Being half carpenter, I did the work myself.

I found, as I'm sure most new parents do, that handling a baby can bring many unexpected traumas. One day about a month after moving to New Orleans, I was watching Chip and he fell off the bed. I can still hear the crack as his forehead hit the bare hardwood floor. I picked him up, thinking I was holding a badly hurt baby. He cried and cried, I think more from the impact of the fall than from serious injury. But I stayed up all night long and watched him sleep to make sure he was okay.

Harriet found out that her widowed step-grandmother lived in Gulfport, Mississippi, which was about fifty-five miles east of New Orleans. Harriet communicated with her, and we were invited for a weekend visit. On our first trip, it was a surprise to meet this little old lady in her eighties who lived in one small room in a hotel. Her only possessions were a hot plate, small chair, table, refrigerator, and bed. Our expectations of hospitality soon faded, and we ended up taking a room in the same hotel. Nevertheless, we fell in love with her, and during that summer we spent many weekends with her in Gulfport.

At work, I soon made friends with another young C.P.A., Trammell Crow, who was the financial officer for the 8th Naval District. We arranged family get-togethers, as we each had a baby boy. When the Crow family learned that we were spending some weekends in Gulfport, they decided to join us, and we spent many outings there together.

When Mr. Higgins found out that I had made a dozen trips to Washington, D.C. to pick up contract checks for my former employer, I soon found myself headed back there again. This time, though, I was travelling on a DC 3 airplane, instead of the usual train ride. Here I was, a kid from North Dakota, flying in an airplane! I was probably the most frightened passenger on the plane.

On my first trip, we ran into a storm over South Carolina and one of the plane's engines stopped running. I was extremely frightened. The pilot was able to land the plane at a little airport, and I was sure that was my last plane ride. By the next morning, however, the weather had cleared, the sun was shining, and the second motor was repaired. We finished our flight to Washington without incident.

On subsequent trips, I traveled with Mr. Higgins. We were getting sizeable contracts with the Navy for watercraft of all sizes, including landing craft for vehicles and personnel, mine sweepers, PT boats, and

Liberty ships. These trips lasted two or three days. On these occasions, Mr. Higgins wined and dined the people he was working with in the engineering, purchasing, and acquisitions departments. I provided the second level of entertainment and took the female secretarial staff, including an occasional male counterpart, to dinner. I enjoyed these outings, but somehow felt guilty eating in some of the nicer restaurants while others were left literally, looking through the windows.

Higgins Industries authorized me to sign checks from the Navy, since I was traveling to Washington so much. One day, a check for twelve million dollars to a supplier showed up on my desk for a signature. I could not believe that a young businessman my age would be given such a responsibility, but that is what happens during war years.

During this time, I also met some very interesting people. One was Kheen Berry, president of the Whitney National Bank, who had been Mr. Higgins' banker for many years. The huge sum of money he was handling for our company engendered his personal interest. We became fast friends.

I worked fifteen or more hours a day for the Higgins Boat Corporation, as did everyone during that time. Workers in this country had not yet heard of an eight-hour workday. Many times I left home in the morning and worked straight through until late evening. Saturday and Sunday were the same.

The company assigned me two secretaries to help with my duties. One secretary was assigned to track the change orders on the Navy contracts, while the other assisted with the accounting work. Since there were millions of dollars involved, both women stayed busy.

Since I spent so much time on the change orders part of my job, I was considered necessary for the war effort. Therefore, every three months, Mr. Higgins would handle another request for deferment from active service for me.

Mr. Higgins introduced me to Preston Tucker, an inventor he had engaged in 1944 to help come up with ideas to shorten the war and carry Higgins Industries into a peacetime economy. Mr. Higgins told me to help Mr. Tucker in any way possible.

A few days later, Mr. Tucker told me he wanted to buy a house that he and his wife had chosen on St. Charles Avenue. Since I had handled big money with the Whitney bank, I helped Mr. Tucker by introducing him to Kheen Berry. Mr. Tucker had a map of the entire property, with a value placed on every tree and shrub. One of the biggest weeping willows was valued at $6,000, which was considered a huge sum. Mr. Tucker bought the house.

Mr. Tucker went on to invent, produce, and market the Tucker car, a revolutionary car that might have been a success if he had the financial backing. According to a movie about Preston Tucker's life, fifty-two of the automobiles still exist in our country today.

One Friday afternoon, Mr. Higgins introduced me to a Navy Admiral with gold braid and many distinguished insignia all over his uniform. Admiral Yates had been heavily involved in the World War I projects, and while he was retired, he had been called back to help the Navy buy watercraft for this war.

Mr. Higgins told me to take Admiral Yates to dinner that night. The Admiral wanted to go to a bar he had frequented during World War I. He knew the exact location and told me to take him there. When we entered, he yelled out a greeting to the bartender, an old friend from the war, and told him to, "Give me the same as you did in the first war." This special drink required a set of three glasses for one drink. The bartender first combined the ingredients in a large glass, poured them into a second glass for shaking, and poured the mixture into another glass for drinking. He lined up seven sets of three glasses each in front of the Admiral and the same in front of me.

That's the last thing I remember until I woke up twenty-four hours later, on the floor of my little living room. Harriet said I had wandered in about 3:00 A.M. and collapsed on the rug, where she left me until I woke. She stepped over my drunken body for twelve hours while I was "dead to the world." I still have no idea how I dropped the Admiral off at his hotel and got to my house without mishap.

My upbringing as a small businessman, which was essentially what small North Dakota farmers were, and first forays in Michigan as a business owner, had whetted my appetite for more. I looked around New Orleans for another venture. During the war years, a lot of people were moving around from one location to another — workers to new jobs, soldiers, sailors, marines and their families from base to base. Two friends and I decided that there would be a great opportunity to have a Mayflower Moving Company franchise in the New Orleans area. The business seemed to fall into our hands, and we soon became the sole franchisee for the area. To add to our business, we added a warehouse and two trucks.

These two men became life-long friends and very successful businessmen. Trammell Crow and Neal Pendleton.

The warehouse operation was simple: just a matter of storing and retrieving people's household possessions. The trucks were another matter. Eventually we bought an over-the-road trailer, for a lot of money, in addition to our smaller truck for local moves. We were always able to find someone who would drive our truck for a few days when they were off of their wartime factory jobs, which took first priority, of course. But it seemed that the drivers we found always ended up with some problem. One time, for example, we received a call from the highway department in Maryland. Our truck had been sitting abandoned on a highway for several days. I could not get away, so one of my partners flew to Maryland, drove the truck to its destination, unloaded it, and returned to New Orleans. He had to take a leave of absence from his government job to save the situation.

Despite my grueling work schedule, or maybe because of it, Harriet had no trouble making friends with a lot of young people. Most of us could not afford to eat at expensive restaurants, so we would go along the wharves on the bayou for evening fun. We loved all kinds of fish, and since restaurants could not serve condiments like catsup, mustard, or olives (because they were imported, these items were not available on the general market during wartime), we always carried our own bottles of goodies.

During these years, we occasionally scraped up enough money to visit some of the outstanding restaurants in New Orleans. I found that Arnaud's was the greatest restaurant for fish and salads. When I landed the job of taking a prominent figure to dinner, we went to Antoine's. My favorite meal was Oysters Rockefeller, Chicken Rochambeaus (a cherry sauce over broiled chicken), and flaming Cherries Jubilee.

Even while off-duty, reminders of the war were everywhere. One

Saturday afternoon a friend and I were driving along the Mississippi River when suddenly we were face to face with three military policemen with guns drawn. There had been a prison break at the nearby German prisoner-of-war camp. The policemen ordered us to get in the back seat while the three soldiers got into the front and drove off to look for the escaped prisoners. Shortly after we started out, we saw another group of military policemen rounding up a small group of prisoners, who were handcuffed while they waited for a military truck to pick them up. We were ordered to stand by until they left.

Helicopters were a new invention in this war, and the Navy assigned a developer, Mr. Sikorsky, to New Orleans. The Navy was so impressed with Mr. Higgins that they wanted this developer to create the helicopter under the supervision and cost direction of Higgins Industries, Inc. I was given the job of determining the cost of engineering and production of this helicopter. At times, I would stand alongside one of these experimental helicopters when the rotors started to turn, and the amount of air blown down on me was phenomenal. I quickly ran to get out of the way.

One day, I was offered a chance to ride in one of these experimental crafts, but I declined, remembering the last time I "test drove" a new boat. Back in Benton Harbor, one of the mine sweepers we developed was ready for testing on one of the coldest and windiest days on Lake Michigan. I went along, a born-and-bred land lover from North Dakota, a state with probably no more than six inches of water. While we tested the 120 foot mine sweeper, the swells were at least ten feet high, and water washed over the deck in two foot waves. I was sure that I would never see my wife and son again. I didn't want to test fate again in a helicopter.

The Senate Investigating Commission began scrutinizing contractors who provided goods and services to the military as the war progressed. One Monday morning I was introduced to Harry Truman, then a senator from Missouri. He had been assigned to investigate Higgins Industries for the Navy war contracts. I made my desk available to Senator Truman for the two-month audit that he conducted. He always wore a dark suit, white shirt, and a broad-brimmed hat. Mr. Truman worked by himself, where today, I think, a Senate investigator would have an army of help doing his job and carrying his suitcases.

As the war in Europe ended in May of 1945, Harriet informed me that we were going to have another baby. It was a time when people were concerned and traumatized over what had happened to our friends, relatives, and acquaintances, and did not seem the time to have another baby. I also knew that we were going to leave New Orleans, and that working in the aluminum industry was my goal.

Harriet was confined to the house during her pregnancy, without any air conditioning, while the temperature was in the high nineties. On January 17, 1946, at 10:00 A.M., she called me at work to tell me to come home and take her to the hospital. I caught a ride home with the Higgins' shuttle, which took me right to my house.

When I ran in, I could see right away that a trip to the hospital was necessary. When I went into the garage to get the car, I noticed that it had a flat tire. It was uncommon to have spare tires during the war, so I quickly took the flat off and ran down to the filling station to fix it. The attendant felt sorry for me and fixed the tire in a hurry. When I arrived back home, we set off for the hospital.

Ann Alvers Noecker was born at 2:30 P.M. that day. What a joy it was for me to look down at that little red face, hardly an hour old. The doctor assured us that she was perfect in every function and every part of her body. I remember Harriet and I stared at her little arms and hands as they flared around in the air. I could not have been happier with this little babe.

Had I known how reliant I would be on this little baby when her Mother became sick with cancer, I would have put a crown on her head.

Remember, we did have our little boy, Chip, who was three and a half years old. Our good friend, Margaret Crow, cared for him until Harriet came home with baby Ann. In those days a hospital stay for a new babe was about a week.

We learned that as soon as a baby girl is born in New Orleans, the parents can register her to be a Mardi Gras Queen candidate. I called my friend, Kheen Berry, and asked if he would sponsor Ann. Before she was forty-eight hours old, Ann was registered as a potential Mardi Gras Queen when she would turn eighteen.

During the war years, Mardi Gras had been canceled. In the spring of 1946, the first Mardi Gras in years was scheduled, and it looked to be bigger than ever. Since I knew we were going to be leaving New Orleans soon, I finagled two tickets so Harriet and I could attend.

We started our night at Antoine's with my favorite dinner, After dinner, we joined the thousands of revelers from around the country on the streets and gathered doubloons for hours. Small gifts, candies, trinkets, and jewelry were among the items thrown by people on the floats to the poor people on the ground.

After the war in Europe ended, I made plans to go back to Michigan and enter the aluminum-window business with my father-in-law. Mr. Higgins asked me to stay until all the Navy contracts were completed and settled, since I had been so actively involved in the change orders for the past three years. I agreed to do this, and stayed in New Orleans until mid-March, 1946.

Before I left, I sold my old Ford, which had served me well, and took the train to Detroit. The train from New Orleans to Chicago was one of the most outstanding trains in the country at the time as it was the first new passenger train built since the Depression. Harriet and I made the overnight run with Chip, age four, and Ann, age two months. Needless to say, we were up all night with the babies. I think I sold the Ford more for the train ride to Chicago than for necessity.

Since no new automobiles were manufactured from 1941 to 1945, it was impossible to purchase a new car in 1946 without a friend in high places. When I reached Detroit, I needed a new car, and contacted a family friend from North Dakota, George Mason, who was President of Nash Kalvinator. To my surprise, he couldn't get me a new Nash, but sold me a new Plymouth two door. I was the happiest Plymouth owner in 1946.

★

My Life's Work

ON MARCH 16, 1946, I STARTED WORKING FOR THE KAUFMANN WINDOW Corporation in Detroit. The 3,000-square-foot factory was located on the second floor of a building on the corner of Kercheval and Hart. Every week he made a very small number of windows, and during the calendar year of 1946, our sales totaled $87,000. This seemed like a small amount compared $400,000,000 brought in by the Higgins Boat Corporation the previous year. This did not deter my excitement, however, and I kept the vision of making a successful business in windows.

Mr. Kaufmann started the company in 1937 after running an ad in one of the Detroit papers asking readers to send him ideas for items to manufacture. One letter suggested making a storm window that could be changed from the inside. Until then, storm windows were big, heavy wooden frame units that were installed from the outside, which often required that the owner carry them up a ladder and put them in while perched precariously two stories up.

Mr. Kaufmann developed and manufactured, on a small scale, a custom storm window, which had removable rails for the half-unit sash to slip into. He also developed the Deluxe model, where the window frame was permanently installed, but the window had both upper and lower glass storm sashes and screens. This was a very flexible arrangement for the homeowner, who could easily adjust his windows for the seasons. Finally, Mr. Kaufmann developed an aluminum screen frame and engaged the Aluminum Company of America to make it. Alcoa representatives have told us that this was the first extrusion (press molded from aluminum alloy to meet specifications) they ever made for the window or door industry.

His business ran into a snag during World War II when the government prohibited the use of aluminum in non-essential products, including windows. Mr. Kaufmann stored his equipment and went to work helping the war effort. After the war ended, he took his machinery and equipment out of storage and began making windows again.

For the first several weeks after I started with the company, Mr. Kaufmann allowed me to wander around the factory getting my feet wet. This piqued my interest in becoming a window man. One of my first sales was a storm window to a home located on Outer Drive in Detroit. The customer was apprehensive of this new-fangled technology and only ordered one window. I was excited about this sale, only to find that the wood window did not have an outer frame. The company had to build a new outer frame with a wooden brick mold around it to hold our storm window. Mr. Kaufmann was very firm in handling my oversight and made me pay the twenty-one dollars for the wood frame. With a commission of eleven dollars per storm window, I lost ten dollars on my first sale! With that lesson, I decided that all units must stand on their own feet and that I would make a profit on each sale.

The first windows we made were made of zinc-coated steel because aluminum was not available for storm windows. During that summer, Mr. Kaufmann and I perfected a framing for the glass that was made on a used, eight-stand rolling machine he purchased.

We found an immediate market that summer for these storm windows, thanks to the federal government. This was when the Federal

Housing Administration (FHA) initiated a program allowing home-owners to borrow money for up to thirty-six months to install storm windows. Since the Kaufmann Window Company was the only storm window made in the area, one of the Detroit banks came to me to begin the program locally. Soon I sold an FHA financed job, one of the first in the area.

The beginning of 1947 was a turning point when we hit on the idea of selling the tools to make storm windows to other people interested in distributing the windows. Without this potential for national distribution, we thought that the storm window business would always be very small. Our program was exactly the same in principle as today's fast food franchises, but it was a novel idea for the time.

We decided to charge $15,000 for a set of tools. I went to work designing the tools with a tool man, who seemed to know what I wanted ed before I did. We duplicated the tools being used in the Hart Street factory. We ran an ad in the Wall Street Journal showing a little man standing on top of the world. This was similar to the look of President Harry Truman standing on top of a wedding cake - then a popular joke. We targeted existing businessmen and told them this would be an ideal business for a son, son-in-law, brother, or father-in-law, or any other relative you wanted to put to work.

Little did I know then how this ad would pilot me to becoming the top-selling window man in the world. This program lasted for fifteen years, and we eventually sold one hundred and twenty-five sets of tools in the United States, thirty-six in Canada, twelve in Europe, and two sets in Africa. Many of the businesses that purchased the tools were jump started into thriving businesses, and some are still known today as leading manufacturers in the field.

In 1947, as the program expanded, we added a storm window for steel casement windows, picture windows, hopper windows, and most other types of windows. In 1951 we hired an engineer to develop an aluminum storm door using the same principles, which we began selling to our dealers around the country and in Canada in 1952. Thousands of these doors were sold, and within several years we were also selling the tools to make the doors from lineal sections of aluminum supplied by the Kaufmann Corporation. Many of these franchise dealers became our customers in the commercial door and entranceway field.

Somewhere along the line, I decided that every Kaufmann aluminum product would have a nametag. We first stuck on the tags with glue, but soon discovered that dealers were scraping off our nametag and putting on their own. So we put a nail hole in each end of the tag and attached one to every product with two drive nails.

Within a few weeks of our first ad for the window making tools, a heating company from Philadelphia was moving into the home-improvement field. Our tool man had just finished the second set of tools (ours was the first), and the head of the Philadelphia company came to see us. He liked our company, our storm windows, and the tool program. He could see the market was ready for aluminum storm windows that could be changed from the inside. So, within a few weeks, we sent him the tools, an order of aluminum, and parts to make a thousand windows.

Soon we also had dealers established in Boston, Port Chester, New York, Washington, D. C., and Richmond, Virginia. This grouping of cities made an easy East Coast swing for me, the person designated to provide the needed leadership to get them started. Since I was young and knew all about the business, I was the one to travel, despite having a wife and two children at home whom I hated to leave. On Sunday night, I went to Boston, Monday night to Port Chester, New York, Tuesday night to Philadelphia, Wednesday night to Washington, Thursday night to Richmond, and Friday back home to Detroit. These five organizations were each already established with good sales teams, and with my help and regular visits, they kept our form machine loaded. I made this trip many times in those first years because our dealers and their roll employers knew nothing about aluminum storm windows and had trouble understanding the product.

To keep up with our dealers' demand for aluminum and everything they needed, we bought another second-hand roll-form machine. This machine was a ten-stand machine, which allowed us to roll bigger sections of aluminum than our first eight-stand machine.

I had had no experience running a retail sales organization, so I stumbled along through 1947 developing an organization in Detroit capable of selling storm windows house-to-house. I decided on this sales method after recalling my college days of selling vacuum cleaners and magazines door-to-door. In those days, vacuum cleaners were a novelty and every housewife was a potential customer. The market was there, we just had to make the sales. In fact, one morning I sold three vacuum cleaners and made as much money in those few hours as I would have at my cashier's job, which was four hours a day, six days a week.

I thought that storm windows were also a ripe market for door-to-door sales, ready to explode like the vacuum cleaner market did a decade ago. I looked for salesmen who had experience in this type of sales to hire. I soon had a force of forty-seven retail salesmen selling storm windows in the Detroit metropolitan area. Our volume and profits increased daily, and we knew we had hit on a product that customers needed and were capable of buying. The results were very good, because, as I explained to the men, they could make a profit of three to five hundred dollars with one storm window sale, compared to a five-dollar profit with magazine subscriptions or a sixty-dollar profit per vacuum.

Selling was not everything. We also had to install the windows we sold. I advertised for carpenters, handy men, and enthusiastic workers. One person I hired was a man with several sons in high school, which was handy because before I knew it, I had weekend crews of high-school boys installing my windows. As a side note, at least six of these high-school installers are still with me fifty years later in some capacity. Some are businessmen in their own right, some switched to installing commercial windows with me, and others are leaders in the field of installing home improvement products.

With five dealers and forty-seven salesmen, our production capacity was soon exceeded and we had to expand into a second plant. Overnight, we were a two-plant manufacturing company. I quickly hired a young "engineer" to help me, and soon found that his previous experience as a bank cashier counting money translated into counting machinery, equipment, tools, and product.

One day the engineer told me he could make me a roll-form machine by buying the parts from various manufacturers. He planned to power it with a car's transmission serving as the "Boston Gear Box." This hand-made roll-form machine worked much faster that I anticipated, and overnight we had purchased a new set of aluminum rolls for the machine to make into our window sashes. This new machine had three speeds and a reverse, just like a car. When working in low gear, we could produce six hundred feet of sash per minute, compared with approximately fifty feet per minute on the Tishken machine. When I was not around, the fellows put it into second gear and even third gear. We could produce more sashes in two hours than we needed in a year.

Business came from all directions. A friend who was a sales manager for a major aluminum company, whose territory was Puerto Rico and Cuba, told me that he was bringing a potential customer from Puerto Rico to our plant. The businessman's beautiful teenage daughter attracted more attention than him during the visit. When we received an order a few days later, every employee wanted to go help the new dealer get established as a window and door dealer - him and his daughter, that is.

Cuba was another matter. My friend suggested that I travel there to establish the dealership, so Harriet and I were soon on our way. Within a few days we had an order for a set of tools. Before we left, we spent an enjoyable evening at Cuba's outstanding nightclub, The Tropicana. Another order we received was for screen porches for twenty-two generals in the Cuban Army, placed directly by one of President Batista's men. I returned to Detroit feeling on top of the world.

We made the screen porches from a drawing provided, and sent them off for installation in the generals' homes. After several years of active business in Cuba, which included some very interesting trips, the Cuban leader, Batista, fell to a revolutionary party. We lost track of our dealer and never did learn what happened to him, his business, or our tools. Perhaps he was persecuted because of his connection with the twenty-two Cuban generals of the previous regime.

Around 1951, when the Korean War began, I became the chief salesman for the Kaufmann Window Corporation. This conflict caused a problem because once again the supply of aluminum was limited for non-essential uses, such as storm windows and doors. Overnight, we were out of business. Not to be outdone, I immediately began switching some of our sections to zinc-coated steel or even full steel for a screen frame and sash. Neither of these two metals worked, however, as main frames for the windows or doors.

We learned that there was a small amount of surplus aluminum around the country available for windows and doors. On Monday mornings, government employees would review the available supplies, and their alloy and thickness. Applying the "squeaky wheel gets the grease" principle, my coworker, Dave Padilla, and I alternated Sunday night trips to Washington, D.C., to plead for our share the next morning. This process kept us in the aluminum window and door business until the war ended two years later, and aluminum was again readily available.

But the war years took a toll. In 1952, we lost $12,000 because of the scarcity of aluminum and the introduction of our new wood window. This was the first and only loss I ever faced in more than forty years of business.

In 1952, Harriet and I took Chip, Ann, and little Bill (who had arrived two and a half years previous) to visit my parents in North Dakota. Bill was learning to use the toilet and we found ourselves miles from any store without any potty chair. This was also before there were any plastic toilet seats that fit over the adult seat. My father, spurred by necessity, took a plain board about twelve inches square, and cut a hole in the middle. He also made a back and sides about four inches high to keep Bill in place, with a strap across the front to hold him. The contraption fit over the adult toilet and was greatly enjoyed by Bill. When the vacation was over, little Bill wanted his potty seat. It was his security blanket, and he would not leave without it. One of my suitcases became the carrying case for a North Dakota invention: a child-sized toilet seat.

On another vacation, I saw some beach chairs made from aluminum tubing. Following my philosophy that you cannot stand still in business, I returned full of enthusiasm to get into the aluminum chair business. I hired Peter Allen, a sales engineer, to help me produce a line of these chairs. Since I had three children under ten in 1952, I wanted to also develop these chairs in smaller sizes for children. We made a rocker and four-legged chair for children eight and under, and five chairs for adults: a rocker, stacked chair, chaise lounge, four-legged stool, and a lazy boy.

We hired Lenore Johnson to market them. Her husband worked for an auto company and she had a brand new four-door yellow Dodge sedan. With a picture of an aluminum chair painted on the side of the car, she sold as many chairs as we could make. Making the chairs required some new tooling, and I bought a Pines bender for $9,000 - a fortune in 1952 for someone with my meager finances. It was worth it as we were receiving calls from as far away as Washington State, where a man came from with his family to sign up as a dealer for the chairs. He also took the storm window and door tools to establish dealerships for those products.

The day the Korean War ended, the chair business really took off. We bought a truckload, 30,000 pounds, of one-inch diameter aluminum tubing, the basic material of the chairs. However, I soon decided that I needed cash to finance my company's growth and that the chair business did not fit our program. I ran an ad in the Wall Street Journal:

> Aluminum business for sale: Manufactured product producing over $250,000.00 volume annually but capable of $5,000,000.00 or higher annually. Business can be moved in four home-moving vans over a weekend. Entry business for your son, son-in-law, brother, father, uncle, or other unemployed relative that you want to put to work.
>
> Telephone: TW-3-2000, Detroit, Michigan.

I received one hundred and five responses to this ad, and forty-seven companies or individuals followed up with a letter. With several purchase offers to choose from, I sold to the Mid-South Manufacturing Company in Tennessee. They came in one weekend and loaded all the equipment and inventory of aluminum and completed chairs into four moving vans.

After writing off everything I could, I wound up with a cash profit of $42,000. This was a lot of money in 1955, especially to a thirty-nine year-old manufacturer who was just a kid from North Dakota. This was one of the best deals I ever made, disposing of an unwanted business and sticking to my field. I am sure that many other manufacturers hesitate to do this when they should.

I kept the profits in a separate bank account for a year, and then decided to buy a Yoder coil slitter. Until this time, we had to buy our aluminum coil with standard slit widths for our sash window framing, awnings, and siding. The slitter paid for itself in a hurry because we could buy painted coils of aluminum thirty-six inches wide, and slit them down to any width and weight. This allowed us to reduce our inventory by at least fifty percent, and allowed us to slit coil each day to the width and quantity needed to fill that day's orders.

My zeal for additional products and expanded business knew no limits. After seeing a jalousie window, I thought that this would be the window of the future. Hugh Buchanan, a cousin of Harriet's who was also my chief salesman and engineer, and I, saw an architect's specifications for a new hotel to be built in Honolulu, the "Princess Kailani." We decided to put together a bid for the hotel's planned thirty-two hundred jalousie windows, although we knew only the contractor's sales person. Within a few weeks, we received a purchase order for the windows, which we had no idea of how to build.

In our hysteria and fright, I went to Florida to see how another company was making this type of window and develop our own unit. I sat on a beach and remembered how a John Deere drill worked back on the farm in North Dakota, using a horizontal rod to open or close an opening. Inspired by that memory, I came up with an idea to open each of the glass units by adjusting a rod vertically up or down. This method worked, and we hand engineered a unit to open and close the windows, which was approved by the architect based on my crude drawings. Today this product and procedure would not be acceptable.

Over the next few weeks, we developed a gear-operated unit to work the windows. We began making the windows and sending them to Hawaii. Many nights we did not sleep worrying about how these jury-rigged windows would be received. Reports came back that they were satisfactory and we continued to make all thirty-two hundred windows. We all rejoiced when we received the final payment, and we never received one complaint about the job. A few years later I traveled incognito to the Princess Kailani hotel and was amazed at the satisfactory and glowing reports on our jalousie windows.

We soon realized that we had another set of tools to sell for others to manufacture and distribute jalousie windows. We sold some fifteen sets of tools to make these windows, and some of our original manufacturers are still making our units.

My frequent traveling continued to bring me unusual experiences. One time I was flying from Knoxville to Nashville to meet with my dealer there. I was sitting next to a bright young man who stuck out his hand and introduced himself as Duncan Rinoldo. I reciprocated, and we began talking for the duration of the flight. When we arrived in Nashville, he excused himself, took a big, black bag from under the seat and headed to the plane's restroom. When he emerged, he was dressed in black - black shirt and pants, and carrying a big holster with a gun on either side. It was the Cisco Kid!

He told me he was helping to open a new shopping mall and that I could come alone to watch. He admitted realistically that he could not imagine why he was such a hero and why parents would bring their kids to see him. As we alighted from the plane, he strapped on the holster, put the guns on each side, and put on a black mask. At the bottom of the stairway, there was a screaming crowd of kids and parents waiting for him. He introduced me as his manager and I probably had my picture taken a dozen times as the Cisco Kid's manager. After a few minutes I said goodbye. I could not wait to tell my television-educated kids about this!

The Kaufmann Window Corporation decided that aluminum awnings for windows, porches, and doors would be another profitable home-improvement venture. We bought a truckload of one-inch square Alcoa aluminum tubing, which filled our entire shipping area at the window and door plant. I hired a bright, young engineer, Robert Yazejian, to develop and market this product. On February 1, 1957, his first day, we traveled to western Michigan to buy sample window, door, and awning stands for our product shows around the country.

Then we bought a thirty-six-inch window awning sheet, the forerunner of the step-down awnings that developed. These sheets sold so well that we bought a thirty-six-inch-wide roll machine. We developed an automatic cut-off machine that allowed us to cut the sheets as needed while rolling a new concept for that width of aluminum sheet in the roll-form field. Over the next two years, we bought another Yoder roll-form machine and developed step-down rolls with a hook lock.

The aluminum-awning business surpassed our expectations of volume, diversity, usability, and sales. We purchased a new Yoder roll-form machine and used it to roll lock-seam tubing. Once we perfected the lock, we rolled millions of feet of one-inch and one-and-a-half inch tubing each year. We added another step-down awning with twelve-inch coverage to our product line, and it took off as a hot seller all over the country.

With the new products, Mr. Yazejian also made the machinery and equipment to sell, using the same tool-marketing program as for the storm windows and storm doors. We also made a deep-throated saw that let us cut the awning sheets up to six feet wide in a continuous strip. We sold dozens of those saws around the country and I am sure a lot of them are still in use. We soon became a leader in the country for making step-down awning sheets.

Shipping the product was a problem as we found the trucking companies extensively damaged the twenty-four-foot awning sheets. Instead of shipping the sheets in small lots, we decided to ship the sheets in truckloads to warehouses around the country. We soon had warehouse dealers in Cincinnati, Cleveland, Chicago, New York City, Boston, Buffalo, Dallas, Phoenix, Atlanta, and Miami, to name a few cities. This had an unanticipated benefit of stocking our warehouses in January, February, and March in preparation for the spring rush, months that typically have low volume. These months now had the same production volume as September, October, and November. We also sold the manufacturing tools to the warehouses so they could cut the awning sheets to size for the local awning installer.

We were soon known as the largest awning-component manufacturer in the country, and our sales reached nearly $10,000,000 during the best years. Our engineering expert, Mr. Yazejian, calculated that we roll formed enough siding and awning materials to go around the equator at least ten times.

Continuing to add new product lines, we also found a market for extrusions in the canvas awning industry. We began shipping extrusions, roll-formed, lock-seamed tubing, and supporting members to this industry.

When we looked at expanding into the European market, we realized that people there were very nationalistic. We approached Reynolds Aluminum Company, our source for coil-painted aluminum, for help making a "Dutch Orange" aluminum sample for our first targeted country, Holland. Soon we were selling these orange and black awnings to all of our European accounts.

For the European market, we developed a roll-up awning that could be lowered when the sun was shining on a window and rolled up when it was not. This was a great invention for us and we received very firm patent rights on it.

The air conditioning industry got started during World War II. Initially, the units were purchased by commercial accounts in very large lots. But as time went on, the industry became our enemy. Air conditioners geared to personal consumers became affordable, and units for a two or three bedroom house cost approximately $2,000, the same as the cost to install awnings. We saw the writing on the wall as our market, both domestic and in Europe, began to slump because people preferred air conditioning to awnings. We sold all of our equipment to a small manufacturer with low overhead who managed to eke out a few more years from this business.

While the awning industry sank, we were studying another product line — aluminum siding. We started slowly in this industry by becoming a distributor for one of the larger siding manufacturers for the first year. Then we decided to go into the business ourselves and purchased rolls to make the various aluminum siding sections. We hit this business as it peaked, and overnight our business took off.

The only issue to manage was distribution, because the very-thin aluminum sheets were often damaged during shipping. We found some warehouses in major cities, and this also increased our business during the slow months of January, February, and March.

Our Chief Engineer, Ken Thorn, developed another set of manufacturing tools for us to sell to dealers around the country. One of his most innovative creations was a section of siding with a ventilator punched into it, providing air outlets at the gables of a house. This one item really helped our success. However, we were soon the most-copied company in the field.

The door-to-door salesmen who sold aluminum siding became know as "Tin Men" in this so-called suede-shoe industry. Selling aluminum siding was a very high-pressure sales job and the stories are legendary. One man told us he obtained a license for his car with the initials "RMC," which stood for Reynolds Metals Corporation. He moved this license to whatever car he was driving that day on his sales route. He even put it on the limousine he had available for his use, embellishing it with a sign indicating that the limo belonged to the Reynolds Metals Corporation. By calling himself Mr. Reynolds, and carrying a briefcase with the company's insignia embossed on it, he passed himself off as the owner. Before he left a home, ninety-nine times out of a hundred, he had a sale from the owner who was so impressed to do business with the Mr. Reynolds.

Over the years, we began to have competition in the aluminum storm-window business. A company could draw a frame, sash, screen, and so on, send it to an aluminum extruder, and after paying a few hundred dollars for an extrusion die, the company was in business.

Although we thought that our roll-form window was much better, it cost tens of thousands of dollars in equipment, rolls, and cutoffs to get into the storm window business this way. With so many new competitors offering extruded windows, the only way we could keep up was to develop and start manufacturing extruded aluminum storm windows. Our largest dealer, Otto Sindelar, who owned Weather-Tite, Inc., agreed to help us. Within a few weeks, Ken Thom had us ready to manufacture our first extruded aluminum storm window. We started another tool program to sell the tools to make this product. The line of fabricating tools we developed sold from between $10,000 and $20,000, depending on the dealer's anticipated volume.

★

Home Life

WE HAD MADE OUR FIRST HOME IN GROSSE POINTE IN MARCH OF 1946, after relocating from New Orleans. This home was a forty-year-old house built during the First World War, and we lived there for two and a half years. Chip had smallpox while we lived there, and Harriet and I were both very concerned for him as he was severely ill. There were some joyful times as well. I had always enjoyed gardening, a love acquired during my childhood on the farm. In the spring of one of our first years in Detroit, I planted tomatoes, peppers, beans, and cucumbers. We all enjoyed looking at this garden as it grew and imagining its bounty. Ann, however, decided that it would be more fun to pull up all the plants one day and uprooted every single one of the hundred we had growing and left them wilting on the ground. To this day, she is the only one of my children who never gardens.

In 1948, Chip started elementary school. We decided to move and bought a nice little house on Meadow Lane in Grosse Point Farms. We lived there for the next seven years, and both Bill and Nancy were born while we lived there.

Chip was a hero on his Little League Team, which was established in Grosse Pointe Farms in 1952 when he was ten. He played in the age bracket for nine to twelve year olds, making the team as a second base-man. Early in the season, he made an unassisted triple play after catching a fly ball, tagging the runner from first base and stepping on second base before the runner heading to third base could return to the bag. One of the local residents was a writer for a large newspaper who wrote up the story, which was published in the paper and in the monthly magazine of the Detroit Athletic Club. For many years this story reappeared and was used to spark the players on the Little League teams.

By the age of nine, Ann was our tumbling expert. She could do cartwheels, body flips and handstands, and always enjoyed the gymnastics classes we enrolled her in. She showed everyone how good she was one night at a PTA meeting in the school gym. A rope hanging from the gym's ceiling had marked points on it that kids in various age brackets could climb for, winning a prize if they made their mark. The mark for Ann's age group was about halfway up the rope, but she easily climbed all the way to the top. She kept doing this time after time, winning all the prizes that the parents had, and intimidating the other kids who hesitated to show their skills when they were so far below Ann's ability.

On August 3, 1955, Harriet gave birth to Nancy Elizabeth Noecker, a lovely, beautiful baby who was a blessing to our family. A few days later, we received some devastating news — Harriet had cancer. No one can imagine my feelings upon hearing this news; I took a nosedive. I could not sleep for nights after learning of this news and neither could Harriet. But it was up to me to keep my fears to myself so I did not upset her. A month after Nancy's birth, Harriet was back in the hospital for a serious operation.

Harriet and I had been married for thirteen years at this time. She had pretty much taken care of our home and children during that time, while I earned a living and was free to develop my businesses. During our marriage, we were very respectful and devoted to each other as husband and wife. I could not think of any problems between us in those years.

She had been the foundation of our home life, and now, with the diagnosis of cancer, I realized that I would have to step in. We were very fortunate to already have our housekeeper, Marie, who helped Harriet cook, clean, and raise the children. Marie was our only confidante in this struggle and we asked her to move in with us. She would care for Nancy, who was only a few days old when she came home from the hospital, but required more care than Harriet could manage.

Our house on Meadow Lane had three bedrooms upstairs — one for Harriet and I, one for Ann, and one shared by Chip and Bill. We decided to make the small library on the first floor into a bedroom for Marie and Nancy to share. Fortunately, a bathroom adjoined the library. I retrieved the twin bed I had made during my furniture-building venture while living in Benton Harbor. After polishing it and buying a new mattress for Marie, we placed it in the room. In the tiny room we also packed the baby bed I had built in Benton Harbor, which the three older children had used. The two beds nearly filled the room, but there was space to navigate.

All of this happened within a few days of Nancy's birth. We quickly established a new lifestyle. At this time, Chip was thirteen, Ann was nine, and Bill just six years old.

After a few weeks with this new arrangement, we saw that Marie could handle the home and four children. I wanted to show Harriet some of the world, and we decided to take a vacation, our first together alone since our trip to Washington, D.C. for a long weekend shortly after we were married. We picked San Francisco as a destination as Harriet had some relatives there whom she had not seen since they came to Detroit for our wedding. During our week's vacation, we decided to stay at the best hotel in downtown San Francisco and branch out from there. We spent an enjoyable day and evening with her aunt and uncle, who lived in a suburb of the city. We also visited with a young cousin of Harriet's, who was also a C.P.A.

While in San Francisco, we enjoyed streetcar rides, the Cout Monument, and discovered that there were many buildings and streets bearing the name of Fremont. I remember having read a story about

General Fremont, who was one of the first to venture across the continent to California. He stuck in my mind because he was a great citizen, and was considered a candidate for President in the mid-1800s. I enjoyed looking up everything named after him during our stay.

People then were extremely interested in gourmet food, and I remember that we went to a restaurant called the Blue Fox which was located near the San Francisco morgue. The food was great and I recommended the restaurant many times over the years.

The next summer we went to North Dakota together for a week to visit my family. This was a great week for us, and we took many walks together through the pastures, looking at the horses and cattle as they roamed. One day a big, red bull with long horns spotted us and came charging our way. We ran as fast as we could and climbed through the barbed-wire fence for protection.

Christmas in 1955 was very memorable for our family. Because of Harriet's illness, making Christmas happen was up to me, and I did all the shopping and decorating for the first time that year. I bought Bill a climbing apparatus like the one telephone repairmen use when climbing a post. Bill's gift had a belt around the waist and a collection of six or eight children's tools hanging off of it, including a screwdriver, hammer, and awls. The apparatus also had an extra belt that could be tied around a post to hold the climber in place, just like the real belts did.

On Christmas morning, we all came down early to open our gifts, me barefoot and in my pajamas. We eventually noticed that Bill was not in the house, and suddenly heard him screaming and crying from the yard. We looked out of the window and there was Bill, dangling by his climbing belt about eight feet up in a pear tree. Although it was a cold morning with about twelve inches of snow on the ground, I ran out barefoot, climbed the back fence, and went up the tree to rescue Bill. I unsnapped the belt holding him, and he fell into my arms. I climbed down and carried Bill over the fence and back into the warm house. This story of Bill's mishap has been repeated Christmas after Christmas over the years in our family.

We decided in 1956 that our house was not working, having Marie on the first floor and the other three children, who were quite young still, on the second. We found a nice house on a nearby street that had three bedrooms and two baths on the first floor, and two bedrooms and a bath on the second. During the past year and a half, Harriet had been in and out of the hospital quite often, accumulating many doctor bills not covered by the insurance I had. I had no business financially buying this house, but under the circumstances, I wanted to give Harriet the best that I could.

In the spring of 1960, Chip graduated from Grosse Pointe South High School, the first student in the school's history to have completed four accelerated classes. While these classes were a great idea, the hard work they entailed limited him to making friends only with the twenty-nine others taking the same classes that year. He did excel in tennis, and by his senior year, was a champion tennis player in the area of Wayne, Oakland, and Macomb counties.

Chip decided to go to Dartmouth and wanted to go there so bad he wrote on his application, "If I don't get in at Dartmouth, I am not going to college." This strategy worked and Dartmouth accepted him. That fall he left for college, a shy young man and excellent student. In October, Harriet and I went to visit him for a Parents' Weekend, accompanied by Dr. and Mrs. Robert Ruthven. We flew to Boston and rented a car for the trip to the campus, which at that time was still an all-male college. We had a wonderful weekend and I thought that Dartmouth was the most beautiful college campus in the country. We stayed at the Hanover Inn, an institution at the time in American college campus hotels. When I returned to Dartmouth seven years later with Bill as a potential student, the Hanover Inn was being torn down and bricks were lying everywhere, a sad sight. I brought home six of the bricks. In my basement workshop I mounted each on a polished mahogany board. I then bought six bronze plaques telling the history and gave them to friends who were Dartmouth graduates.

During the winter of 1961, Harriet and I decided to vacation in Jamaica where we had vacationed several times in the past. Because Jamaica is the source for a lot of bauxite, a basic ingredient of aluminum, two of the largest aluminum producers in the world had entertained us on the island previously. This time would be different as we were going to tour the island according to our own plans and schedule.

We spent four or five days at each of three outstanding vacation hotels. One day we met a traveling judge from Great Britain, who was sent once a year to Jamaica to review local cases and handle those involving serious crimes, such as murder or rape. We spent a whole afternoon with this fascinating man, who told us many stories.

We learned that the island is one place in the world where pimento plants thrive and that much of the world's supply came from one area. We took a side trip to a primitive factory in this area where the berries were processed and the juice squeezed out.

Another day we visited a sugar-cane plantation. The stalks of sugarcane were eight or nine feet tall, and the area was very aromatic with a sweet smell. We watched dozens of men cutting the tall sugar-cane stalks in a rhythmic way, their movements like music. The men threw the cut stalks onto a wagon, piling the load as high as possible. Then six or eight oxen strained at their yokes to pull the heavy wagon to the processing plants. The oxen were also like symmetry in action.

We took a new Kodak camera on this trip, determined to capture everything — even the birds that ate from our hands as we ate breakfast on the balcony of the beautiful hotels. We felt we could "sell" our collection back home. On our last day in Jamaica, we piled our luggage at the restaurant door with the camera bag on top, after being assured everything would be safe. After breakfast, we went to collect our belongings and found the camera bag and all our film and paraphernalia gone. With just an hour until our plane left, we did not have time to even report the crime. We realized the thieves planned it this way, knowing they would be safe.

During the years I was taking care of Harriet, I also had a business to run. Fortunately, I had always required less sleep than most people, and I did a lot of work at night. My right-hand man was Dave Padilla, who lived near us in Grosse Pointe. Night after night, Dave came over at 10:00 P.M. after Harriet, the children, and Marie were asleep, and we would go over business plans for the next day, week, and year. I certainly would not have been able to maintain my business without his help, as well as that of Bob Smith, Ken Thom, and Bob Yazejian.

From her diagnosis in 1955 until 1961 we had no idea of how severe Harriet's illness was. For six years, we struggled from hospital to hospital, church to church, and from psychic to psychic. Many people who have cancer live for many years in a remission, considering themselves cured. This is what we always hoped for. Anyone who has gone through the cycle of cancer knows about the ups and downs, where the downs are very low and any bright spot is a very high sign. Harriet and I certainly had our share of this roller coaster ride. But we did not win.

By the middle of 1961 we had tried every possible avenue to find a cure. Doctors finally told us that recovery was impossible.

My doctor decided that he should tell Chip and Ann, who were then eighteen and fourteen, that their mother was not going to recover. The doctor came to our home to tell them that he could not save their mother. He, too, was very attached to Harriet and I learned later that he cried while discussing the situation with Chip and Ann.

The end for Harriet came on September 13, 1961, and I was forced to make many decisions, though I was in no way prepared for all these considerations. A person never thinks that the end will come for a loved one.

First I had to tell Bill, who was in the sixth grade and had no inkling that his mother was so ill and might die. That Wednesday morning I went to his school to tell him that his mother had left us, and to bring him home. This is probably the hardest and most wrenching thing I have ever done in my life.

I had to return to the hospital to sign a death certificate and a hospital release form for the body. Next, I had to choose a funeral home. In just a few minutes, I had gone from enjoying the touch and love of my beautiful wife and mother of my children, to helping them manage a body that they wanted out of their building in a hurry. I walked out of the hospital in a stupor.

I stopped at a funeral home I had driven by for years. The director was pleasant and started to rattle off the services they had to offer. It had only been an hour since Harriet stopped breathing. I told him I wanted a respectable "laying out." Then we went to choose a coffin, taking an elevator to a second-floor room filled with dozens of empty coffins. It was an eerie feeling to choose a coffin and it reminded me of going through my first cafeteria line at college, trying to determine what I wanted to eat. After I chose a coffin and signed several documents for him, he suggested that I visit my minister.

Reverend George Kurtz had baptized all four of our children and confirmed Chip and Ann. Also, I had been treasurer of the church for five years. Harriet had been one of his favorite people and he visited her regularly when she was in the hospital. He told me that I had to choose a cemetery and recommended a new Lutheran cemetery thirty miles away.

The cemetery's caretaker was very helpful and when she learned of Harriet's young age and that we had four young children, she really went into high gear. I told her that I wanted a hillside facing west, just like the Fairview Cemetery in North Dakota that my grandfather started. We found just what I wanted, and again I had to sign papers plus hand over a check. The thirty-mile trip home seemed easier as I felt I had chosen something that Harriet would have wanted. It was just 4:00 P.M. and I had made a lifetime of decisions.

Just before the service, the funeral director asked me to decide what to do with Harriet's rings. During the viewing, she had worn a diamond ring and the wedding ring I gave her in 1941. The diamond ring was made from a large diamond that her step-grandmother in Biloxi, Mississippi, had given her. We had made this ring into an engagement-style ring with two diamonds on either side. He suggested that I remove both rings, but I decided to remove only the large ring and leave our wedding band with Harriet forever.

The next few days were the most devastating of my life. Hundreds of people came for the viewing on Thursday and Friday. Ann and Chip were steadfast in their support. Harriet had told Ann it was her job to keep me on an even keel, and she did not let me out of her sight. Friends from all over came by, from church, the Little League, the Young Presidents Organization, neighbors, Harriet's school "buddies," and her relatives. Everyone offered help and I was not alone. If it sounded as if I was alone on Wednesday, it is because the duties and obligations I had to undertake were of such a personal nature that I wanted to handle them myself.

The funeral was Saturday morning at the St. James Lutheran Church, which was filled to capacity and overflowing with mourners standing in the narthex. God gave Harriet a beautiful day for her funeral, recognizing her as a wonderful person who led an exemplary life. I cannot describe my feelings at the cemetery as I watched the coffin being lowered into the grave. The rest of the day is a blank to me.

Many years later, Reverend Kurtz told me that Harriet's funeral was one of the largest he had ever officiated at during his career.

My brother Raymond, and his wife, Delphine, arrived on Thursday to stay for a week and help run the family and household. I appreciated this so much. They were both take-charge people and on Monday morning they suggested that they remove Harriet's personal items and clean out her closet. I was very thankful for this, as it would have been very heartrending for me and the children to do.

My brother and his wife returned to North Dakota the following Saturday morning and I was alone with the children for the first time. About 10:30 P.M. the children were in bed and I was sitting alone in the living room — probably with a martini — feeling desolate. I heard a faint knock at the door and found that my friends Bob and Eileen Maier had stopped by. They had driven by several times, saw my lights, and decided to stop. This was the best thing that could have happened, and I often think of it as the bridge that got me from one life to another.

We quickly established a regular routine without Harriet. Our housekeeper, Marie, continued to stay with us from early Tuesday morning until late Saturday evening. Then Molly, our laundress, took over and cared for us on Sunday and Monday until dinnertime. Every Sunday we all went to church, reflecting my strict Lutheran upbringing in North Dakota. Afterward we went to Baskin-Robbins for an ice cream treat.

I arranged with a neighbor girl to take Nancy to first grade every morning and bring her home after school. I paid this girl fifty cents a day for these two errands, which perhaps now seems like too little for such an important service.

To make the household run smoothly, I made some very strict and firm rules for everyone.

1. We would eat dinner every night in the dining room on a white tablecloth.

2. I would not allow a ketchup bottle, milk bottle, or mustard jar on our breakfast or dinner tables. Milk was served in a pitcher, ketchup in a dish, and mustard in a respectable container with a spoon for serving.

3. All of the children, even Nancy at six years old, had to hang up their towels and washcloths in the bathroom.

4. All dirty clothes must be thrown down the chute, not left laying on the floor or around their rooms.

5. All the children by age ten had to make their beds every morning, all year round.

6. Work was mandatory. Chip mowed the lawn in the summer and shoveled snow in the winter. When he went away to college, Bill, seven years his junior, took over. I also encouraged Chip and Bill to take every lawn-mowing and snow-shoveling job they could get and Ann to take every babysitting job she could get.

7. Each child could have a dinner guest every other week.

I decided that I must have humor, frivolity, and fun in the house, and that I must teach responsibility, loyalty, and respect for other family members. These, plus many other character traits were on my mind, as the sole parent, to teach my children. In a two-parent household, there is the temptation to think that things are the other parent's responsibility. I believe that a single parent, especially a father, takes his responsibilities more seriously than a parent does in a two-parent household.

I wanted my children to have a constant reminder of what I valued, so each month I printed a saying on a shirt cardboard and put the sign on the refrigerator. These eight-by-fifteen-inch signs gave them our family message of the month, such as:

1. With privilege goes responsibility.

2. Pray for a good harvest, but keep on hoeing.

3. Manners month.

4. Employment is a noble occupation.

5. Respond to a compliment.

6. Success is a journey, not a destination.

7. The Fear of the Lord is the Beginning of *Wisdom.*

8. Neat and Clean Month.

9. You get more with *Love* than *Hatred.*

10. In the *Family* as in the *State,* the Best Source of *Wealth* is *Economy.*

11. The First *Rule* of this home is *Discipline.*

12. Be Happy!

13. Learn to Accept Rejection.

The kids and anyone who visited our home always commented on these signs, with the most comments being for "With privilege goes responsibility." I still have all of these shirt boards in one of the kitchen cupboards and occasionally bring one out when the children and their families come to visit. I have even seen signs in some of the children's homes, posted for their own children.

Every night as I was driving home from work, I tried to think of that night's dinner-table conversation. My daily goals were to have three topics that we could all discuss that would interest the children. This was important to me because my parents always wanted us as children to express ourselves. One day, I hit upon the idea of having the children express themselves extemporaneously on a subject for a minute or two. For example, Chip could talk for two minutes about college, Bill for two minutes about his Little League team, Nancy one minute about sidewalks, and Ann for two minutes about elephants. The rest of us would listen attentively during the talks.

We did this exercise about one night a week, most often when a child had a guest for dinner. At first it was hard for the kids, but then they gradually began looking forward to their turn and what their subject might be. Today, I know that all of my children can express themselves in a group, which is a tremendous asset to have.

★

Moving On

BY THE TIME 1963 ROLLED AROUND, I HAD RECOVERED MY COMPOSURE and began adjusting to Harriet's death. I was handling the many responsibilities of being a mother and father to my four children, and getting on with business.

We bought two companies that year, the first an extrusion company that had one small press. Our production volume with extruded aluminum windows and doors was so great that we had to move back a step in the manufacturing process by producing our own extrusions. This was an interesting, small purchase for my company because we bought the entire business, including receivables and payables, which I had until then avoided. We also were fortunate to have Glenn Hustead join us with this purchase. He became a valued, trustworthy, and innovative employee for many years.

Next, we bought the Brasco company of Monroe, Michigan, which made extruded commercial doors, commercial entranceways, and fixed walls made of aluminum extrusions and glass. This product line fit right in with the extrusion press I bought earlier in the summer. Both purchases strengthened our presence in the aluminum window and door field.

Chip and one of his friends from the Little League team worked for me that summer, both now eighteen years old. I also hired a young Greek man as a full-time employee when he was just eighteen, and the man considered himself indebted to me for life because I helped him out with a personal problem. I took all three of these young men to all purchase-related meetings of these two companies. Many years later I kept hearing about how wonderful these experiences were for them at such a young age. George Gazepis is one of my most valued coworkers some thirty-five years later.

Europe!

I LEARNED EARLY IN MY CAREER AS A CPA THAT IT IS BETTER TO TAKE earnings and invest them in your business, not declare that money as profits and pay taxes on them. Between 1957, when I paid off my original investors, and 1959, I was able to set aside $10,000 to develop my franchise tool program in Europe.

In 1951, when my father-in-law, Harry Kaufmann, passed away, I was left as the manager of the Kaufmann Window Company, which was a sizeable organization. In early 1952, with investors, I purchased the assets of Kaufmann Window Company from the estate. Business was very good.

In 1957 I paid off the investors and changed the name of the company to Kaufmann Window and Door Corporation. A good friend and business associate, Trammel Crow, pushed me to use the name

"Marshall Noecker" so that people would recognize the name of the company, and so I did.

In November 1959, John Buse, a citizen from the Netherlands, called me on a Friday afternoon from Toronto. For the past few months, he had been living in Canada and successfully selling storm windows for one of my dealers who had bought the tool program to make aluminum storm windows. Mr. Buse told me that he wanted to come to the United States and sell windows for me. However, he did not have the permits required to come into the country and asked if I could come to Toronto and discuss this possibility with him. Harriet was too ill with cancer at that time for me to go, so I asked my storm-window sales manager, Bob Smith, to go. Always a cooperative person, Bob agreed to go on Saturday morning to meet with this gentleman.

On Monday morning, Bob came into my office wearing a huge smile. He told me that John Buse was a character. Bob found him living in a cheap hotel, just finishing his laundry so his underwear, socks, and shirts were hanging over the bed from temporary clotheslines strung between the brass bedposts. The room had only one chair, and since the bed was full of laundry, Bob sat on the floor while they talked — probably the only deal we ever made with our sales rep sitting on the floor.

Bob told John that his plan to come sell windows in the United States would mean he was no farther ahead than any other sales person in a very competitive field. Bob soon discovered that John had some money saved, the equivalent of $10,000 in American dollars. Playing on the man's ego, Bob told him he could be a Dutch entrepreneur by using that money to buy our tool program and become a storm window manufacturer in his own country. John liked this idea and said he would be going home for Christmas and would discuss it with his family, who lived in Blariscumb, Holland. When Bob left Toronto Sunday, he had a verbal agreement with John to become a manufacturer in Holland. John's agreement was unusual for a resident of a country where normal, common citizens rarely become manufacturers.

I arranged a three-week tour of London and Europe, part business, part vacation, for Chip, Bob Smith, and me. We wanted to establish dealers for our aluminum storm windows in London and Europe, and also have some time to see famous sights.

We arranged for a day of sightseeing in New York City because we were catching our flight to London from there. We left for New York on December 26, 1959. The next day we saw the sights in New York, including the Radio City Rockettes and the Empire State Building.

At the airport we learned that we would be flying to London on a four-motor jet, a type of plane that had only been flying for a short time across the Atlantic. We all were concerned about flying on this new type of plane. I remembered a promotion about the plane that said the wings flex up to three feet while flying — they were built to do that. With this fact fresh in our minds, we soon hit storms over the ocean. I was absolutely petrified when I looked out of the window and saw the wings flexing up and down in the torrential wind. Bob and Chip were also frightened, but they had something else to worry about — motion sickness. Both were very sick to their stomachs all night, until they had nothing more to throw up. This was probably the most unpleasant night of any of our lives. When the sun came up in the morning and we could see the ground below, it was the greatest sight. We alighted in London without incident, probably three of the most frightened people who had ever crossed the Atlantic. I thought of Charles Lindbergh crossing the Atlantic in his little plane in 1927, all alone skimming the waves, flying in the dark.

A bus met us at our airplane on the runway and took us to the terminal. Getting our baggage and going through Customs took quite a while. At Customs, our bags were opened and searched with a thoroughness I have never before experienced when traveling to Cuba, Puerto Rico, Jamaica, or Hawaii.

While we were completing this process, Bob discovered that we could take a bus to the downtown London station for much less money than a cab. We enjoyed this unexpected saving. Next, we took a cab from the station to the Dorchester Hotel, one of the better hotels located on one of London's nicer streets. We checked in, and each of us took a long nap, all exhausted by our fright, sleeplessness, and sickness. We awoke in the evening, ready to see the sights.

Chip had done his homework on London before we left Detroit, and had a list of thirty-six places for us to visit while we were there. Our first stop was the Marble Arch, which was just across a park from our hotel. As we neared the arch, we came across dozens of soapbox orators expounding on their theories of life, love, and the world. Speakers had only a few listeners who were mainly heckling them. We listened to the hecklers in the park until after dark. We also got our first sight of London Bobbies, the local policemen. The Bobbies wore a dark uniform, a helmet-like cap, and carried only a nightstick for a weapon. We figured the armored cap was to protect them from assault with a club.

We then walked toward Trafalgar Square. It began snowing in heavy, wet flakes, making our first sight of London after dark a beautiful thing. At that time, the square was lined with old-fashioned gas lamps. We watched a man in a red smock coat, carrying a ladder and a torch, light each lamp. He would lean his ladder against the lamppost, climb up, raise the chimney on the streetlight, and light it with his torch. We took pictures of this unusual and beautiful scene before heading back to our hotel.

We had four or five days for sightseeing, and after a good night's sleep and a big breakfast, we began tackling Chip's list, which now had thirty-four items left on it. I found the Tower of London most interesting. I had read over the years about Henry the VIII disposing of his many wives in that tower and was eager to see this infamous place. We were met at the tower's door by Beefeater guards. Although we looked like typical American tourists, we each were very curious about the tower and did not hesitate to ask many questions of the guards. We had many wonderful conversations with the Beefeaters and I believe that we were shown many items and scenes not usually shown to the typical tourist.

We gazed at all the torches, mechanisms, and the tools used to behead the various wives. We were amazed to find that the cells had been maintained in the same condition as when prisoners lived there. The beds, sleeping accommodations, and food dishes were still arranged in the cells.

Our next stop was Big Ben, where we were awed by the clock's beautiful, soft, sweet-sounding chimes. After that was St. Paul's Cathedral, where we wandered among graves in the ground and walls of people who had died centuries before. For history buffs, this was very interesting.

Throughout our sightseeing ventures, Bob and I were also attending to our real reason for being in London — establishing an aluminum storm-window dealer. We spent a lot of time looking at newspaper ads and calling people who we thought might be interested in our program. We did not find anybody who would even talk seriously with us about going into business for themselves in this field.

On the afternoon of New Year's Eve, we flew to Paris for the next leg of our trip. When we arrived at the Orly airport, we saw three or four large Russian Aeroflot planes on the tarmac. We were worried for our safety, thinking maybe we were in hostile territory, until someone told us that the "rich" Russians came to Paris to celebrate New Year's. We learned later that "rich" meant privileged members of the Russian government, not wealthy like Americans would think.

We stayed in Paris in a small, four-story hotel a half mile from the Arc de Triomphe, arriving again on a snowy night. After eating, we walked the length of the Champs-Elysee Boulevard, to the Arc de Triomphe and back. We were surprised at the width of this famous boulevard. We learned that Napoleon made it so wide, even tearing down buildings on one side, so many people could watch his triumphant military parades as he conquered Europe.

Paris came to life in the darkness, and we saw people parading around in fancy clothes and disguises. They found somewhere in Paris' history the most outlandish costumes to wear for the New Year's Eve celebrations. We returned to the hotel, but I decided that this night I would explore the city. Bob declined and went to bed. Chip was too young, so I went out alone to see the world.

I had heard that Pigelle was the place to be and headed there in a cab. The place was coming to life when I arrived, an American alone, fairly well dressed and clean, with a supposed large American billfold to match. As I strolled along, I was offered company for the evening every ten feet. This amused me after the first batch of propositions and I enjoyed a lively conversation with each woman that approached me, though I declined all their offers.

At about 11:00 P.M., I decided to go to a nightspot. The one I entered surprised me because it was simply a large, empty room. The maitre de greeted me in French and I answered in English. Neither understood the other, but before I knew it, he had unfolded a little table, about sixteen inches in diameter, and unfolded a chair to go with it. He motioned for me to sit down, and not knowing what else to do, I sat. A waitress offered me a drink, and I gathered that only champagne was consumed in Paris on New Year's Eve. I established the price and said, "Bring it!" I soon had a bottle of clear champagne in an ice bucket on my little table, with a wonderful pedestal champagne glass in front of me.

Before I could take my first sip, the maitre de came over leading twenty-five rather large men and women in large, bulky clothes, especially their coats. I thought this was my first view of French peasants from the countryside, but soon realized that I was surrounded by a group of the "rich" Russians. After we all had had enough champagne to be relaxed, we became great friends for the evening.

I also learned that the reason the room was empty when I arrived was that the maitre de brought tables to fit the size of the group arriving. There were tables for one, two, four, and up to ten people, which the Russians were using. By 11:30 P.M., the room was full.

At midnight, I was surprised to hear Auld Lang Syne being played. The Russian women immediately pulled me up to dance with them and we were soon swinging around in wild style. I was forty-four years old, and these women were slightly older, but probably rarely left their country and were determined to celebrate this great night. They all pressured me to go back to their hotel with them, but I was cautious, and had enough common sense to decline and bid them farewell.

When I left the nightclub, I watched the line up of revelers arriving and leaving. Those arriving came on small motorbikes, with a man driving and a woman on the rumble seat. They would park their bike, lock it, and then change their clothes. The man would take off his helmet and his heavy coat and end up with a suit, tie, and white shirt. The woman would take off her heavy coat and mud shoes, and slip on her stockings and high-heeled shoes. The transformation from motorcycle rider to nightclub attire amazed me. They all did this changing in a small shed outside of the nightclub's main entrance, perhaps built just for that purpose. The people leaving the nightclub reversed the process.

At that time in Paris, cars were uncommon as the country was still suffering from the after effects of the war. Everyone used motorbikes instead. Another lasting effect of the war was the continued scarcity of silk stockings in Europe. Almost every woman I talked with asked me to send her silk stockings from America. I took many names and cards, but no one ever wound up receiving a pair of stockings from me.

After I left the nightclub, I decided to wander around some more. It was well after midnight and I could not believe that a kid from North Dakota was wandering around Paris enjoying the nightlife on New Year's Eve. I walked for hours, watching the thousands of people celebrating and roaming the area with painted faces. Champagne was the drink of the evening, although I am sure these people were drinking the three-dollars-a-bottle kind, not the twenty-dollar-a-bottle champagne the rich French people drank.

I arrived back at the hotel at 6:00 A.M., only to be greeted in the lobby by a young lady wearing a tan mink coat. She offered to be my friend for the weekend. While I was not afraid of wandering around by myself, I did fear French women, and I went to bed alone. Before leaving her, she told me that her best friends were airplane pilots from around the world. Fifteen minutes later, I watched her meet a pilot who just arrived at the hotel and took her up on her offer. I remember thinking that I should have been a pilot.

Chip woke up when I returned to our room and told me of his own adventure. Each hotel room had eight buttons, each summoning a different service offered by the hotel. A drawing by each button told you what they were; for example, a little man with a tray represented food, a lady with an ironing board was a person to press your clothes, and a person with shoe-shining equipment was someone to shine your shoes. Chip did not realize what these buttons meant and pressed them all. Soon there was a knock on the door and the first service arrived to his room, summoned by the button. Chip suddenly understood what he had done, but he had only two American dollar bills, which he gave to the first two servants who arrived. After that, he was embarrassed by having to dismiss the other six without even a tip. He told me that he would never again push a button in a hotel room!

I went to bed and slept until noon, when we all decided to go find something to eat. All the restaurants were closed because it was New Year's Day, but the city's bakeries had stocked long loaves of French bread and bottles of red wine to feed the starving people on the holiday. We did not realize all this at first, and walked into a restaurant and sat at a table, waiting to be served. We soon realized that we were on our own, and then noticed a couple with two young boys sitting nearby with several loaves of bread and bottles of wine on their table. We asked them where they had gotten their food, and in French we could hardly understand, they told us that down the street a small bakery was selling the bread and wine. Chip and Bob went to buy our meal and soon returned with three, two-foot-long loaves of bread and three bottles of wine. I decided that if those little boys could drink on New Year's Day, then so could we.

After eating, we walked around the general area of the Louvre. We watched dozens of artists along the street painting portraits of tourists. We were tempted to join the waiting crowd, but decided it would be better to see the Mona Lisa than to have our portraits painted.

When we approached the Mona Lisa, we all stood in awe, looking at what the French considered the greatest painting in the world. She had a smile that has never been captured again in a painting, and that every woman could want for her own. The rest of the Louvre contained an outstanding array of pictures. Outside of the London galleries we had toured, it was an impressive collection of art to me.

Toward evening, we decided to tour the Bastille, the infamous French prison where many atrocities had taken place over the centuries. The prison was no longer there, instead only a statue featuring a one-hundred-foot-tall spear, topped by a winged person pointing south. We all laughed at the missing prison as Chip had had it as one of his sight-seeing goals.

The next day we headed for the Eiffel Tower, which was an awe-inspiring sight to a boy from North Dakota. Chip and Bob, not being tired like I was from my night on the town, energetically climbed the stairs as far as they could up the tower. I sat on a bench to rest instead and learned my own lesson about French postcards. Street vendors marked me for an American and approached me with their wares, the postcards that were a predecessor of pornography. Most of the cards were in envelopes, but I was smart enough not to buy anything I had not seen. So I made them show me their wares. I did buy a packet from them, and I still have one of the best pictures today.

The next day we targeted Notre Dame and other places in the area that Chip thought were worth seeing. As we admired the cathedral, it was hard to believe that it could have been built eight hundred years ago, without any modern equipment. We could not imagine how these stones were lifted forty, fifty, or sixty feet into the air and notched together so well that they were still standing today, not a stone moved. We had each read about different types of architecture and recognized that the cathedral was built using the flying buttress principle. I tried to teach my son some of what I knew about the building industry while we looked at the cathedral. We also enjoyed looking at the fantastic interior.

Throughout all of our sightseeing, we continued to take our meals from all different areas of the city. Street vendors were everywhere with loaves of French bread and their wine, which became the staples of our diet while there.

Bob and I also spent some time answering ads that we had placed in a Paris newspaper looking for a storm-window manufacturer. We had much difficulty communicating with these potential French window dealers because they knew as little English as we knew French. I still remember Bob speaking one word at a time, in his slow, direct manner, trying to impart his meaning. With each word he would get louder, thinking it would help them understand. It never did.

We finally gave up on establishing a French connection and moved on to Amsterdam, where we were not complete strangers. John Buse met us and took us around to see the sights for a few days. We spent a week with John and finally went to his hometown of Blariscumb, a town about twenty-five miles south of Amsterdam. We saw many men, women, and children all wearing wooden shoes, which was a novelty to us. The climate was very cold, partly because of the high humidity of a country surrounded by water. In Holland, you were walking below sea level, and we were amazed to see a ship anchored in one on the many canals where the water was twenty feet higher than the street.

We left Holland with a check from John for $10,000, his initial tool order. We also agreed to give him a similar amount of inventory so he could start making windows — our first European dealer. We returned home to Michigan on January tenth, smug and happy with our first foreign manufacturing business.

We had agreed to return to Holland after the tools and inventory arrived and help John get started. We shipped the tools in March, and took the next jet to Amsterdam after John notified us that they had arrived. We were taken aback when we saw the building he had chosen in Blariscumb for his manufacturing facility. It was approximately twelve feet by twelve feet, and our lineal window material was twenty feet long. There was eight foot of material hanging out of the window, supported by wooden sawhorses. John had covered it with canvas to keep it dry.

We began hooking up the tools. Since we had sold more than one hundred sets of these storm-window tools in the United States and Canada, Bob and I quickly had everything set up, and began making sample products. John and his son, John Jr., helped out. John Jr. was a young man in his early twenties who lived in a small apartment nearby with his wife and one or two small children. Within two days, we had John and John Jr. set up as manufacturers. Hundreds of neighbors surrounded the little building and watched us make aluminum windows because the process was a novelty to them.

Before we left Holland, we wanted to help John install a window on an actual opening. We gave the manager and owner of the hotel we were staying in a storm window for his building, which we installed before returning to Michigan. Within a few weeks, Bob had an order for enough materials to make another hundred storm windows, which supplemented the original order. The Dutch people were very cautious, and in most cases ordered just one, two, or three windows for their homes to test the product.

As I mentioned earlier, one of the main sparks for our storm window business in the United States was FHA financing for home improvements, giving homeowners money to buy storm windows for their whole house. In Holland, there was no such financing available, and owners had to pay cash for their windows. Many times, John set up a plan for homeowners that bought and installed two storm windows every three months until the home was complete.

We learned that in Holland the word for storm windows was difficult to pronounce, so what we call storm windows are called piggybacks. John decided to call our aluminum storm windows piggybacks, coining a new name for our product in the European market.

With the breakthrough in Holland, more dealers were established in Europe, and by September of 1960, we had storm-window dealers in Belgium, Scotland, Ireland, and England besides Holland.

The name piggybacks stuck in these countries, and even today storm windows are known generically as piggybacks. In addition, the Europeans called our company insignia KCIO, instead of our KCO after the Kaufmann Company. They pronounced KCIO very fast and it became the trade name for all Kaufmann doors and windows made for the European market.

E l e v e n

Home for
the Holidays

THE RUSH OF CHRISTMAS WAS UPON US. CHIP HAD JUST COME HOME FROM
Dartmouth for the Christmas holidays, and all the children were excited.

Our family was somewhat unusual in certain respects. We had been
feeling our way along for the past eighteen months since the death of
our mother and wife. Our household and most of the needs of the children were handled by Marie, who had "lived in" for the past seven
years.

Nancy was a seven-year-old, second grader, with enthusiasm and
determination envied by all. Bill, a robust, athletic thirteen year old,
was interested in all life had to offer. Ann, our gem, saw to the needs
of all the children while keeping a guiding hand on her father. At twenty, Chip was a junior at Dartmouth, majoring in a five-year business

and engineering course that culminated in a Master of Business Administration (MBA) degree.

Something happened that holiday that altered all of our lives. It started at dinnertime one evening when Ann said a friend was interested in going to Governor George Romney's Inaugural Ball. It sounded like a great idea, and I volunteered to be the chauffeur. Ann's friend was to pick up the tickets, but things went astray when she left them in her desk at school, which was locked up for the holidays. Not wanting to disappoint the girls, I went out to get another set of tickets. I succeeded, but it was tough to shell out five dollars a ticket when the first set were complimentary.

New Year's Eve had been a late night, and so New Year's Day passed without much activity. However, I anticipated the time it would take two sixteen-year-old girls to prepare for their first Inaugural Ball, and told them we would leave at six o'clock when the starting time was really seven.

Ann began dressing by five o'clock. She had chosen a black velvet sheath and she looked beautiful. Her friend, Clare, came in about six thirty in a gold evening gown with a bouffant hairdo. And, as anticipated, she immediately advised me that she was there to put the finishing touches on with Ann. I was long ready to go, dressed in a black business suit, and was idling the time watching television.

About a quarter to seven the girls appeared, as chic and elegant as any young ladies who have ever attended a ball. It took only a look from one to the other and I knew I was not dressed for the occasion. Yet, it took Ann to say, "Father, I thought you would be wearing your black-tie outfit tonight!" And Clare, "Oh, Mr. Noecker, let's go all the way." So, back to the bedroom I went. In ten minutes I came out dressed in black tie and got the exacting approval of my two sixteen-year-old "dates" for the evening.

The temperature was nearly zero, with snow and ice prevalent. The girls put on their cloth school coats, and I noticed each carried a stole on her arm. One was white rabbit, and the other squirrel. After some teasing of the two "queens" of the evening from brothers Bill and Chip, we got in the car for the hundred-mile ride to Lansing.

As we arrived at our capital, it soon became obvious that parking was to be a problem. I wanted to pass by the entrance and let my girls off, but they would have no part of being left without an escort at such a gala event. After some driving, we found a parking space only a block away. With the cold, it then became a question of how to handle those two pieces of animal, the rabbit and squirrel. The cold soon spread to the girls' feet as they became timid about wearing their "girl's best friends." But I would have none of it, and carried the skimpy rodents over my own arm. Finding the coatrooms full, I carried my and their cloth coats back to the car.

We soon discovered that the Inaugural Ball, Michigan style, is not one, but three events. In one auditorium the "hep" under-twenty crowd was swinging and swaying in stocking feet. In a second ballroom was the more sedate crowd of middle to upper class — the dowager in her evening dress and the over-plump gal with her fastidious, round and balding spouse. We then learned that the third dance was going on in the basement auditorium and, of course, to get a proper perspective we had to see this, too. There was a small stage, and two loud and enthusiastic bands with female entertainers holding fort. The over-crowded dance floor was close to the stage and populated with some rather enthusiastic dancers who had learned their wiles and ways from instinct rather than Arthur Murray. The rest of the large room was filled with picnic-type tables and folding chairs, where Michigan cherry pie was enjoyed.

It was quite obvious to my girls that I didn't belong at this party in my black tie, and neither did they in their furs and gowns. The girls wanted to step out with the "hep" group, and felt that I should not be watching them, and would be more at ease with my round and balding contemporaries. However, before we could join our separate groups, it was a must to see our Governor.

A scream alerted me to the fact that my girls had spotted the Governor in ballroom number one, along with nine thousand other celebrants. As we crowded in, Governor Romney soon became engaged in his first struggles in what has become known as his "Thursday morning citizenry," namely, dancing with all the girls within his reach for a few seconds. This was a real hubbub — women screaming, stepping on one another, and fighting their way to a dance with the state's number one public servant.

We soon decided that this was no place to attempt victory as a group of three, and I retired to the sidelines and told the girls to fight their battle with vigor. I occasionally glimpsed Ann pushing toward the Governor, and then he would turn and dance with the girls facing him. After nearly half an hour, she succeeded in dancing thirty seconds with Michigan's most popular man. Her friend accomplished the same feat.

Now, what was Mrs. Romney doing when the Governor was dancing with the female population? Well, she was dancing with the male population, and the girls were sure that I should enjoy the privilege of partnering a potential first lady of the land. But I would have none of it. They went on to the "hep" party and I stayed on the sidelines watching for dignitaries and friends (of which I saw few).

It wasn't long until the girls were back at my side with Ann commenting, "Father, we can go home. The evening is complete. We have danced with the Governor." At midnight we decided it was time for the Cinderella slipper to fall. It had been quite an evening for girls of sixteen. The outstanding part was dancing with the Governor, and my girls immediately became his best supporters for the Presidency, for the single reason that if he succeeded, they would be able to tell their friends that they had danced with the President.

Now, as we stood at the door to leave, it became apparent that they would freeze to death going out to the car. I suggested going back to the car for their coats and mine, but they would have none of it as they had met some pretty nice boys at party number two who were standing nearby to wave goodbye. So, to the car we went, waving and freezing.

The Birth of My Political Career

CHIP WENT BACK TO DARTMOUTH, THE OTHER CHILDREN WENT BACK TO school, and I returned to work, soon forgetting about our glamorous evening at the Inaugural Ball. On February 1 I received an invitation to a party from Dr. Bruce DeSpelder, a department head in the Wayne State Business School, and a good friend. That evening, my host kept my hand filled with a glass and jokingly kept referring to making my heart light and my mind flexible. He soon manoeuvred me into a corner and told me that the Republican Party was looking for a candidate to run for the Board of Governors of Wayne State University in the April 1 election.

My immediate reaction was that I had no interest whatsoever as I was both father and mother to four children, the president of eight corporations, and with no official affiliation with the Republican Party.

The evening passed, and about a week later Dr. DeSpelder phoned saying that the Republican convention was being held in Grand Rapids on an upcoming Friday and Saturday, February 12 and 13, and would I accept the nomination to win? Again, my answer was "no." Again, I went about my busy life of business, family, and social activities.

On Thursday morning, February 11, my friend called again, this time asking me to have lunch with him and the Republican Chairman of the Seventeenth Congressional District. I felt that no harm could come from this, and we decided to meet at a downtown restaurant. I had in my pocket a photograph of myself as well as a resume. It could be that my efficient secretary had slipped these into my hand. Anyway, before we reached dessert, the Republican Chairman asked me for a photograph and a resume and said that I should be in Grand Rapids by ten o'clock on Friday morning for the convention. I was scheduled to be in Chicago on Friday and Saturday at the Home Improvement Show, which for years had been an opportunity to meet with my long-standing customers. My decision was final. I was not a candidate. I did not have the time.

I got up early on Friday and boarded an astro-jet for a thirty-two minute flight to the windy city. My sales managers and I spent the day visiting our Kaufmann Window and Door exhibit at the show, as well as touring competitors' booths. By evening it became apparent that I had covered what I needed to, so I made arrangements to catch a 1:00 A.M. plane back to Detroit.

I arrived home on Saturday morning about three, and was sleeping soundly at eight fifteen when the phone rang. I heard Marie down the hall to my bedroom door to say that there was a long-distance call. With my son eight hundred miles away at college and all my family living in North Dakota, I am always startled by a long-distance telephone call. I hurried to answer. The caller was a member of the Republican team in Lansing asking me if I would attend the convention. I went back to bed, only to have the telephone ring withing another half hour. This time I was told that Governor George Romney wanted me for his candidate. I had an acquaintance with the Governor through my membership in the National Young Presidents Organization (YPO), whose members became presidents of one-million-dollar corporations before their thirty-ninth birthdays. Five years before, as program chair, I had arranged for Mr. Romney, President of Nash Motors (later American Motors), to speak at one of our programs. There was an impelling spark from that initial meeting, and over the years we had exchanged waves and hellos when our paths crossed. Then, some two years before, I had been appointed to the Wayne State Businessmen's Advisory Board of which George Romney was a member. I realized that it was possible that the Governor wanted me as a Republican candidate. However, I refused and went back to bed.

Shortly thereafter the phone rang again. I answered this time and was informed by Dr. Bruce DeSpelder that they were going to put my name before the congressional district delegates. I was told there were four or five other candidates seeking the delegates' support, but that the Governor wanted me. At this point, I mellowed to the thought of political life.

Anyway, I went off shopping for the week's groceries, only to find when I returned home that the Lansing telephone operator had been trying to reach me. With calm determination not to be swallowed into this political world, I unloaded the groceries and went to my bedroom to call back. It was my Republican friend. "It looks as if you are going to get this nomination," he said. "Therefore, you'd better get in your car and come up here." It seems that my resistance must have been breaking down as I agreed to leave immediately and be in Grand Rapids by four when the balloting was to take place. To be there in three hours I had to really move. My Ann had other plans, Bill was out with the boys, and I was certain among my girlfriends that it was too late to call and have someone accompany me. Therefore, I set out on the drive by myself.

It was two minutes to four when I pulled into the parking lot in Grand Rapids. I decided to sit in my car to hear the four o'clock news, and to my amazement, heard the newscaster announce my name as the Republican nominee for the Wayne State Board of Governors. A cold sweat immediately came over my hands and forehead as I realized that I must give the speech which I had been haphazardly preparing during the three-hour drive.

I crossed the street and entered the lobby on unsteady feet. Approaching the main door, I saw two, big, good-looking men walking toward me at a fast clip to inquire if I was Marshall Noecker. I realized that my picture had been enlarged, duplicated, and circulated throughout the convention crowd of four thousand.

My big "bodyguards" told me that they had instructions to bring me to the stage. At the same moment, I realized that George Romney was talking on the platform, and I objected to an entry during his speech. My "boys" told me that we would go to the stage, so, down the aisle we went. As we reached the stage, I am sure that I have never felt weaker, and that there has never been a launching of a politician with the sunken feeling that overcame me. As I began climbing the platform steps the Governor was closing his speech. As we reached the top step, he said his last word, and the crowd of four thousand rose in unison to clap and cheer. The Governor stepped toward me with hands outstretched.

Had the stage directors of Hollywood had this assignment, they could not have done better than my split-second entry into political life capitulated by the Governor's outstretched hand. In customary fashion, the Governor then raised his hand, the crowd silenced, and he introduced me as the legendary candidate elected as the last member to their Republican state ticket for the spring election.

Quickly, I was introduced to the other candidates, who were complete strangers to me. In fact, among the estimated hundred people on the stage, with the exception of the Governor, there was only one other face I recognized. That of his beautiful and charming wife, Mrs. Romney. People whom I had never known threw their arms around my shoulder for a picture. There were dozens of cameras and even television news crews. I was completely taken aback, and without ability to comment very intelligently. However, I decided that a word with the first lady was appropriate. As I approached her, she extended her hand and I knew that she perceived my physical and mental status of the moment.

As I left the parking lot, I glanced at my watch to see that in less than forty-five minutes I had entered this new phase of my life which would come to dominate me and my family for the next seven weeks. Driving back to my home, I was overcome by the elation of being brought into this life, and laughing to myself as I anticipated the reaction of my children and friends to my news.

Our first official meeting was on a Tuesday, February 17 in Lansing at the Republican headquarters. I called my running mate to make the trip with me, as I had read his name in Sunday's paper, as well as my secretary, Muriel. My running mate, Dr. Whitaker, came down his steps as I approached the drive to his spacious home in Grosse Pointe, only a few blocks from mine. As he opened the car door and extended his hand in greeting, I knew that my campaigning would be pleasant and educational.

Up until this time I had not realized that there was such an office as Republican headquarters. As we arrived, I remembered not a man from my Saturday afternoon on the stage in Grand Rapids. But I soon realized that the person of Arthur Elliott, Jr. represented the leader of the office and the party.

We — eight or ten candidates and the same number of workers — all sat around a long, conference-type table. As the various speakers stood and gave their programs I must admit that most of it went through one ear and out the other, as political programs were completely foreign to my mind. I tried to size up the candidates to determine their qualifications and their political acumen. The morning passed rapidly.

It was on the walk from headquarters to the YWCA for lunch that I learned that some of the men around the table were not Republican party workers as I had assumed, but were campaigners for some of the candidates. Realizing this, I immediately felt a drive to line up some helpers for myself.

Muriel had spent a busy morning becoming acquainted with the staff at headquarters, taking notes, organizing information, and generally becoming quite adaptable to the program.

Lunch passed without much comment, and we walked back to headquarters where we spent the next half hour having our pictures taken for literature which the Party was going to print for us. Next, it was announced that we would discuss the campaign budget. As we were seated around the table our Chairman threw out a figure of $90,000 as the base for the spring election. I was surprised at the figure and volunteered questions as to where this amount of money had come from, since the Party had carried out an all-out campaign only the previous November for Governor Romney's campaign. My question was answered to the effect that I just be glad we have it, and in politics you don't necessarily ask where the money comes from. Money is raised after it is spent in most cases, as I later learned, and the various county and district chairmen raise it. Then someone announced the division of this $90,000. Each of the two Supreme Court candidates were to get $10,000, and the University of Michigan, Michigan State, and Wayne State University Board candidates would be given $1,250.

We were then shown the type of literature and publicity that the Republican Party would put out on our behalf. This included, in my case, a five-by-seven mailing card with a picture of the Governor, my running mate, and myself. However, we were told that these would not be ready for ten days, which would bring us into March, and of course, the election was April 1.

As we left Lansing, Dr. Witaker stated that he would like to stop by and call on a medical group in the area. As we visited, I learned of the high regard the medical profession held for Dr. Whitaker. I could sense that his candidacy would receive a lot of support, and I only wished that I could ride on his coattails. I had anticipated spending the rest of the week at my desk taking care of business, and at home taking care of my children. Such was not to be the case.

On Wednesday morning I received a call to go to Wynadotte for a Lincoln Day dinner. I took down the address and said I would be there. As the evening approached, I realized how tired I was and did not particularly want to make this trip. However, I talked with my good employee, Robert Yazejian, the Sales Manager of my siding and awning companies, and as I do not like to make trips by myself, he agreed to drive me. We chatted during the twenty-mile drive, and then looked for the bowling alley where the dinner was to be held. I had anticipated a gathering of twenty to forty. To my amazement, there were acres of parking lots and thousands of automobiles around the place. It was then that I realized we were at a major political rally. Stunned, I said to Bob, "If I start running for home, tackle me and hold me."

As we entered, we realized that the speaker of the evening would be Congressman Gerald Ford, representing the Grand Rapids area. As we looked out across the room, I saw seats for as many as one thousand. It then dawned on me that maybe I would be asked to speak, as the welcoming committee knew my name and handed me a lapel sign.

I could not eat, wondering whether or not I would be asked for comments. But, as I sat, I thought of a few things to say, which I estimated would take three to four minutes. As the program began, my hands began to perspire and my face felt flushed. After the toastmaster had finished introducing the local political figures, he turned to the table where I was sitting and announced he was pleased to have a candidate on the State ticket as their guest, and could he say a few words to the group...

I rose, totally unprepared, and believe I made the best political speech of the ninety-one I was to subsequently deliver in this campaign. Since I had no political experience in Michigan, I realized that I should tell these workers that I was a life-long Republican and admit that this was my first venture into the political world. I realized it would be good to thank them for supporting me at the Grand Rapids convention. I made both of these statements in a humorous vein, saying that I had been "a life-long Republican and, as such, had no adversity," and was surprised to see the smiles. Then I told them that I was a widower with children and would like to share a few words about these children. These comments became a legend in my campaign.

"I have four children. Marshall, twenty, is a junior at Dartmouth College, so I know what higher education costs. Ann, seventeen, is a high-school senior, so I know what spaghetti straps are. Bill is thirteen, and I have taken my turn at coaching Little League baseball. Nancy, at seven, is in the second grade and thinks that if I win this election we will move to the White House and she will get Caroline's pony, 'Macaroni.'"

The applause as I left the podium was very satisfying, and I felt this was the approach to make. That people were more interested in me personally than they were in any prolonged statement of opionion on the affairs of the State. As the meeting broke up, I was tapped on the shoulder by several business associates who told me that I had said just the right things. As I rode home with Mr. Yazejian, I was quite pleased and happy, yet astounded by the prospect of five more weeks of campaigning.

As we drove, the question of hand-out literature — something to leave with people to remember my name — became a paramount item of discussion. I said that the Republican party needed ten days to get their literature out. So, the next morning we called our company advertising agent, Ted Wolf, and in few minutes he was in my office. Next came the question of what to say on a formal piece of hand-out literature that we could have within twenty-four hours. During the meeting between Mr. Wolf, Mr. Yazejian, and myself, the statements I had about my children came into the conversation. Mr. Wolf immediately jumped on this and we laid out a card that I thought would tide us over for a few days. Little did we know that this card would become the backbone of my political literature. At the same meeting we decided that we must have a program. A program involves literature, financing, advertising, publicity, mailing, and personal appearances.

I might say that when I returned from my Lansing meeting and realized some of the other candidates had workers, I called a few of my long-standing friends whom I thought could not possibly turn me down, or turn down an opportunity to work on a campaign at the state level. I found that they could and did turn me down.

So, my strategy committee became Ted Wolf, Bob Yazejian, Lenore (the former sales manager of my aluminium chair business), and Muriel. We sat around and decided that since none of us had any political experience, we would tackle this problem the same way we would tackle a sales problem. We decided to find out how many daily newspapers there were in Michigan and how much it would cost to run an advertisement in each paper once a week. A few days later Mr. Wolf came back with a figure of $500. Remembering the $90,000 budget and that political money was spent before it's raised, we scheduled one advertisement in each of the fifty-two papers for three Fridays in March.

Mailing was our next topic of discussion. We decided that we should mail approximately fifteen thousand pieces of literature, which at four cents each would cost $600. This would be the card from the Republican headquarters carrying my picture with Governor Romney and Dr. Whitaker. In mailing to a home, the best catch would be the husband and wife, or two voters.

On the other hand I realized that if I mailed to a filling station with one desk, but six to fifteen employees walking by, we would have a much larger coverage. Therefore, we secured the addresses of the six thousand filling stations in Michigan. Twenty-one thousand cards also went out to the smaller restaurants in the state.

The issue of raising money is one that floored me. At our Lansing meeting I heard candidates throw around figures of $5,000, $8,000, and $22,000. Those numbers seemed out of my reach, so I set a budget of $4,000 which included $600 for postage, $1500 for newspaper advertising, $500 for printing, $350 for advertising to special groups, $150 for radio tapes, $250 for political mats, $250 for costs associated with lining up friends to address cards, $350 travel expenses, and $50 miscellaneous.

Next came the question of how to raise this money. As we sat at the table, my telephone rang with a call from Robert Huber from the Young Presidents Organization. He volunteered to contact that group for me.

As I hung up, Mr. Yazejian agreed to contact my suppliers and customers. Lenore wanted to bring in my relatives, and in accordance with the instructions from Republican headquarters, business and church friends are two other sources of revenue. Before the morning was out, one of my church friends entered my office and I assigned him his job. A business associate to whom we had given some good publicity was asked to contact my business friends. My requests for contributions were covered.

Since we were devising our program based on sales principles, we decided to print envelope stickers, similar to air-mail labels, that we'd had great success with in the past. In was our intent to get a free ride on a lot of envelopes by asking supporters to use these stickers. This became one of our best moves, as we reordered stickers three times for a total of fifty thousand. To get the same coverage in a mailing, the postage alone would have cost my campaign over $2,000.

We finished the session by ordering window stickers, roughly three-by-four inches, stationery, and envelopes which announced my candidacy. Thus, in one meeting we had formulated a political campaign. It had been my thought that each candidate had a campaign manager, a finance manager, a publicity manager, and was loaded with people who swarmed his office to help. I had done it in a morning, with four people inexperienced in political life, but with a determination to present a good fight.

The next day my telephone was ringing in my office when I arrived, with an invitation to the Detroit Engineering Society from the Dean of the Business School at Wayne State University.

When we met, the round of handshaking began with deans, assistant deans and professors. It was at this meeting that I first learned what real political handshaking was all about. Each person that I was introduced to seemed to have some special little story to tell me about his college or department.

I was soon given to understand that all of Dr. Clarence Hilberry's (the University president's) staff were very enthusiastic about his and their accomplishments during his ten years at the helm. The president is supported by people representing the alumni and various associations. Also, by a group of vice presidents, including for medical development, graduate studies and research, finance, administration, and provost government. I soon learned that there are eight colleges in the University headed by Deans — Business, Education, Engineering, Law, Liberal Arts, Medical, Nursing, and Pharmacy. There was also a Dean of Social Work, and a Director of Monteith College (a special liberal-arts program).

As we talked, I realized that it would be a good idea to have a little knowledge of the duties and responsibilities of the board of governors. So, without direct questions and direct answers, but following conversations, I listed what I thought the duties were. These included finding a replacement for Dr. Hilberry and three vice presidents who were all retiring; planning classrooms, faculty, and housing for the flood of new students expected in 1967-1968; investigating development of new branches of the University; upgrading the University from teaching to full status, and adding to the faculty; promoting discussion on athletic programs; and doubling the enrollment at the medical school. This was not a complete list, nor necessarily the most important tasks, but rather a working document to which reference could be made.

During the course of our campaign, I was surprised at how often this question of duties was raised. In the thirty seconds or so allotted for answers, I was always able to draw on this list.

As our meeting at Wayne State continued, I realized that a history of the University would be very useful to have as a ready reference during the campaign.

Upon direct questioning, I was given a birdseye view of the history of this great institution. In 1868 a private medical school was organized by doctors to meet Michigan's need for physicians. In 1881 a normal school to train teachers was established.

The Detroit Junior College began offering a general two-year college program in 1917, followed by The Detroit College of Medicine and Surgery coming under legal control of the Detroit Board of Education in 1919.

The next year the Detroit Normal School changed its name to Detroit Teachers College, and in 1924 the first degrees were awarded. The College of Pharmacy was also organized that year. The Detroit Junior College was similarly replaced by the College of the City of Detroit, which granted its first four-year degrees in 1925.

In 1933 the College of Engineering and the Graduate School were established, and the six existing colleges were united, by action of the Detroit Board of Education, into a university called the Colleges of the City of Detroit. Frank Cody, Superintendent of Schools, became the first president, and the next year the name "Wayne University" was adopted.

The law school, first established ten years earlier as Detroit City Law School, was brought into the University in 1937, and the School of Public Affairs and Social Work was organized. In 1945 the College of Nursing (which began in the College of the City of Detroit) became a college within the University, as did the School of Business Administration.

Wayne University became Wayne State University under Act 183 of Michigan Public Acts of 1956. The next year the Institute of Labor and Industrial Relations was established (sponsored by Wayne State University and the University of Michigan) from the 1946 Wayne University Institute of Industrial Relations. The Detroit Institute of Technology transferred its students, faculty, and programs into Wayne State University's new School of Pharmacy, and the Division of Adult Education, also jointly sponsored by Wayne State and the University of Michigan, was established.

In 1958 the Graduate Division of Instruction and Research replaced the Graduate School, and the Monteith College was established. In 1960 the Institute of Continuing Legal Education was established, to be operated by the law schools of Wayne State University and the University of Michigan in cooperation with the State Bar of Michigan.

The following year Wayne State University and the University of Michigan entered into a dual-election agreement so that students could study at both institutions without additional fees. The college of Medicine also joined with five leading Detroit hospitals to establish the University Medical Center.

To supplement this information, I decided that I should have some data on the students. It was from this session that I learned of a student body of twenty-one thousand. Over ninety percent were graduates of high schools in Wayne, Oakland, and Macomb counties. This was occasioned by the fact that there was little or no student housing on the campus.

In other words, the students lived at home and commuted. Over eighty percent of the Wayne State graduates still lived in Michigan. Therefore, it was obvious that this great University carried much worth in the State of Michigan. I learned that just over fifty percent of the student body was married, and that the average student's age was somewhat older than students at other state universities.

Many of the Wayne students took classes part time, and carried full-time jobs. At this point I considered myself well supplied with facts and information, and also with many new acquaintances who undoubtedly would become fast friends should I be elected to the Board of Governors.

I soon found out what scheduling of candidates means. My calendar for the week arrived in the mail from Republican headquarters. Friday evening was capped by a six o'clock dinner in Paw Paw, put on by the Van Buren county party group. I asked Bob Yazejian to drive me to the dinner, and then to Lansing for a Saturday morning breakfast with the County Chairman.

As we motored westward, we became low on gas and stopped at a station. I had read and heard how politicians got votes along the way. So, as we drove up to the pumps, I took a handful of literature and walked into the station.

I was surprised to find a half-dozen men standing around the waiting room on a cold afternoon. With some hesitation, I talked about the weather, and then got up my nerve to mention my campaign as I handed out the flyers. As I talked, I could see smiles on their faces, and even though they told me they were Democrats, I received the word that they would vote for me.

One elderly man stood up and said there were eight votes in his immediate family, and that if I would give him eight pieces of literature, he would see that I got eight votes. I shook his hand and thanked him.

On arrival in Paw Paw we learned that I was the first candidate of several expected. Mr. Romney was soon to arrive, as the principal speaker for the evening. I was told that after dinner I would be called upon for the customary three-minute speech.

As I ate, I recalled some twenty years ago as a young Certified Public Accountant, I was assigned to the audit of a local winery. As I got up to speak, I mentioned that I felt right at home in their agricultural area as I was born and raised on a farm, and that if there were any cows to be milked by hand that night, I could still do it.

Then I mentioned my experience as a young boy auditing one of their grape wineries, and the old story of sampling the wine in the evening and then taking a drink of water in the morning, one could be happy all day long. I wound it up with a few statements on who I was, the job I was seeking, and that I expected to win only with their help on election day.

As I sat down to applause, I knew then that politicians must personally reach their audience to garner their support.

At the end of the evening Mrs. Romney headed a receiving line that all the guests passed through. It was at this meeting that I learned a politician can shake hands with five hundred and four people in one hour and six minutes.

Bob and I then headed for Lansing and a good night's sleep.

We were up bright and early and found our way to the Republican breakfast in our hotel, the Jack Tar. Here again I was allotted my three minutes (which I exceeded). My plea was to get supporters to help line up votes for me. I passed out my little envelope stickers and asked them to hand them out to as many businesses as possible to use on their mail.

By the time I left Lansing, I had requests for nearly ten thousand more stickers. I felt that we had made a dent into the political arena, and that I had exposed myself to a large number of voters in the state, all at one meeting. I concluded that these state meetings were very valuable.

The next week's schedule listed several meetings in Detroit, including an introduction at the large downtown Rotary Club. Although I did not have a chance to talk that day, I knew that I was reaching a good many friends who would carry my campaign legend to voters in the city.

That same evening my daughter, Ann, was anxious to go with me to a dinner in Jackson. We were seated at a table with Mrs. Romney and the rest of the candidates.

This meeting was slightly different than many I attended because Mrs. Romney acted as the toastmistress. The first person that she introduced was my daughter, who was initially taken aback. Ann retained her poise, stood, and smiled beautifully. Her presence had won me a lot of support, and I knew that a beautiful girl can be a real political asset. I also knew that she should accompany me wherever possible.

A series of coffees was scheduled for the next day in the Lansing area. Women kept coming and we kept being introduced. When I was asked to give a speech, I mentioned that the graduating classes from Michigan high schools exceeded eighty-seven thousand in 1962, and were projected to increase to one hundred and thirteen thousand in 1963, and one hundred and forty-four thousand by 1964. The reason these figures were growing in such rapid numbers in three years is that these were the babies that were born after the war ended.

I was surprised by the interest these figures created with these young ladies, many of whom were mothers with children in their teens or younger. This theme became the basis for my speeches throughout the day.

In the late afternoon my schedule directed us to an ice cream parlor in a town nearby. The owner surprised me when he said my audience would consist of some forty high-school students who were in various booths in his establishment. I found that it was much harder to reach a group of high-school students — interested both in food and the opposite sex — than it was to reach their parents. I did my best, but am sure that I did little to create a desire for higher education in this audience.

After we left, I conversed with Ann, a junior in high school, at length as to what I should say to the future crop of potential college students.

I must admit that I didn't have the answer, nor was she able to supply me with it. Our next meeting with a high-school principal and school board member turned out to be one of the highlights of my campaign in discussing educational philosophy, procedures, and the future of our schools. I was only disappointed that my audience was so small. However, at the end of our discussion, two janitors who had been listening in walked over and said they would vote for me. I again realized the value of reaching the voters. Ann and I then drove back to Lansing for a brief rest and dinner.

The evening was devoted to a gathering of Lansing Republicans, with Arthur Elliott, the state chairman, as the principal speaker. I was given my customary few minutes to project my candidacy, and again realized the value of having a beautiful daughter with me as Ann passed out my literature and spoke with almost every audience member as they arrived. When I was introduced as her father, I am sure it made little difference what I said. Ann already had won their support.

As we drove home, Ann and I discussed the fact that we had appeared in front of ten groups of people, and that this represented a mighty good day for any politician.

With three weeks left until the election, I realized that my business had seen very little of me, and that I could not take my children along very often to campaign as they would have to leave school. Being a widower, I knew several lovely widows who would like to spend a day campaigning, and one in particular who had mentioned it. So, I called Betty for a day in Oakland county.

We started the day with an eight o'clock press conference — breakfast with reporters from four papers, and my fellow candidates. We then set out for "coffees" at three lovely homes in as many hours. The subject was higher education and I talked about our fast-growing community colleges, and the need their graduates would have of finishing their courses at our state universities.

I was surprised to learn that when students left rural communities to attend four-year programs, they rarely returned home. The way I saw it, the community colleges would provide higher education to students who would then become local leaders. This was the theme for the morning, and it was enthusiastically received.

In the afternoon we were scheduled for another series of homes. Then our dinner took us back to Devon Gables, the restaurant where we had started the day. Six of us candidates were assigned a small room for shaving and cleaning up.

The hall our dinner was held in was so full that not another person could have crowded in. Afterwards, we continued on to two more meetings where Governor Romney was the principal speaker. By this time, I was an old hand at campaigning and the audience of nine hundred at the Birmingham Community House did not faze me.

As we finished our last meeting at about ten thirty, Betty and I were completely exhausted. I had stood before three thousand people, and knew that the day had been well spent. I was sure that Nixon and Kennedy had not worked harder in any one day than I had on this day.

The next evening I was scheduled for a meeting in Macomb County. Chip was home from Dartmouth for spring vacation, and to my surprise and pleasure, volunteered to be my chauffeur for the evening. Bill was anxious to make his first political debut, and my two boys did a marvelous job of handing out literature. When I was introduced, mention was made of my sons, and I know that their presence helped to reach the hearts of those voters.

Over the past month I had had hundreds of letters of all sorts. If one looked personal, I opened it. Otherwise, it was tossed into a box. There was just not time to look at it all. And as I opened my schedule on Sunday, March 17, I realized that my week, was again, completely taken.

I was to be in Kalamazoo for an eight-thirty breakfast the next morning, and decided to get up at four thirty to make the drive. Leaving home without breakfast to drive the 150 miles was a mistake. When I reached Kalamazoo, I was exhausted, and my first stop was for a cup of coffee. Then, on to the Kalamazoo Gazette for an interview. We candidates hardly ever saw what the paper printed about us, or the pictures that they published, as we were usually miles and miles away by the time the papers hit the streets.

Lunch was at the Rotary Club in Hastings. The toastmaster told me that there were only two Democrats in the club, and neither were present. Therefore, I could speak for a few minutes to the seventy-five Republicans. During one of my early trips to Amsterdam, our

European dealer, John Buse, took me to that city's Rotary club. These Dutch people are great salesmen, and before I knew it, I had joined. When the Republican party learned of my membership in Holland, they scheduled me for many Michigan Rotary luncheons.

By this time I had gathered some good political jokes. I must admit that the best storyteller of our campaign group was Judge Richard Smith, candidate for the Supreme Court. I had latched onto many of his tales — for example: When success is your goal, keep your eye on the donut, and not on the hole — and used them mostly when he was not present.

It had snowed and sleeted all day, and in the evening I climbed into my car and headed 150 miles north to Traverse City. The roads were terrible, and when I arrived about nine o'clock, I found that I was the first candidate to check into our motel. By midnight there were six of us, plus Arthur Elliott, our state chairman.

Our schedule called for boarding a plane bound for the Upper Peninsula the next morning. We met early for breakfast, even though we had been notified that our plane was delayed because of the weather. Arthur Elliot kept going back and forth to the telephone, and pretty soon he came to tell us that although he had been told that the plane carried seven people, they hadn't counted the pilot, and therefore, only six of us could go.

We were going to draw sticks or toss a coin, but after much hilarity, I was the one chosen to be left behind because I was the youngest candidate in that group. The plane finally arrived and they took off. My instructions were to call Lansing, and they gave me a day as full of political commitments as any that had been scheduled weeks in advance. My first stop was to be in Frankfort, a small, Benzie County town.

The roads were completely ice covered. I drove along at fifteen miles per hour and arrived too late to meet my host at his office. When he returned, he took me to the local restaurant where I shook hands and met the editor of the local paper. I was soon to learn that I was the first Republican candidate for a state office to visit this city in many a year. Later my host and the editor sent me a tally of the Benzie County vote, and to my surprise, I was one of the leading vote getters.

After two more stops, I arrived back in Traverse City in time for a six o'clock radio interview. After the interview, the newscaster introduced me to the station owner, Les Biederman, who turned out to be one of the most interesting figures I had met during my political campaign. He invited me to dinner and told me that he owned four other radio stations in northern Michigan, and that my interview would be played on all of them.

Mr. Biederman had a pet project, namely, bringing a student from Pitcairn Island to the community college in Traverse City, which he helped found. I recalled that Pitcairn Island had something to do with the story of *Mutiny on the Bounty*. His program for the potential student called for raising one thousand dollars to be contributed by listeners to his radio programs in amounts not greater than one dollar each. (After my return home, I sent Mr. Biederman four checks in the names of my children.)

I then went back to my motel to learn that my colleagues had all been snowbound in the Upper Peninsula. We were scheduled for a seven-thirty breakfast, and I was advised to distribute literature for the candidates and to talk for a few minutes about each. I had lived so intimately with these men for the past few weeks that it was an interesting task to tell their stories. Frankly, by the time breakfast was over, I concluded that a fellow candidate or friend could possibly do a better presentation than the nominee himself.

My fellow candidates rented a car and traveled through the snow and ice all night, arriving back in Traverse City at about 5:00 A.M. After some rest, we continued with a full day of events. That evening we went to a six-county Republican rally at Shanty Creek Lodge, where the snowfall had created a winter wonderland. As I was the first candidate to arrive, I asked the manager for the privilege of campaigning with the employees. He gave me the run of the place, and I soon found myself in the kitchen talking to the staff of twenty who were preparing our meal.

Our dinner was in the main dining room with about two hundred and fifty in attendance. Afterwards, we went to a downstairs auditorium where the crowd doubled. Governor Romney was our first speaker, and I again gave my five-minute speech. (Notice that I had been granted an increase from three minutes.) At the end of the evening one of our candidates and his wife discovered that they had no suitcases! The parking attendant had gone home with their car key in his pocket, and their belongings were locked in their car for the night.

The next morning I made three stops across the state. In one small town there were only four businesses — a gas station, a restaurant, a general store, and a place which I never did find out what was sold. I covered the four stores and talked to a total of seven people.

My next stop was Atlanta, where I was welcomed by the chairman of Montmorency County. At lunch I talked with a group of businessmen before proceeding to the courthouse to meet the prosecuting attorney, county clerk, and sheriff. I had covered many county buildings and realized that most of these people were Republicans. A handshake would undoubtedly bring support from a few other voters along the way.

Then we went on to visit a factory which employed about twenty-five girls making screens for the auto industry, before stopping by a supermarket. Again I shook hands and gathered votes. I learned that people on the street looked with awe when we introduced ourselves as candidates. After stops at a bank, newspaper office, and a radio station, I headed for Detroit.

Friday, March 22. I can remember thinking that it was my only sister's birthday, and for the first time in many a year I was so busy that I had overlooked sending her a card or gift. My office, after my four-day absence, was loaded with work that I wasn't interested in biting into. I knew that I should be working on my campaign, and wondered where the weekend would take me.

About noon I received a telephone call from Judge Richard Smith, who had arrived in Detroit after a rally in Alpena that I had missed the night before in my haste to get home and see how the children were doing. We agreed to meet at the Detroit Athletic Club. On arrival, I learned that the Judge had lost the principal button on his suitcoat, and for those of you who have suffered this experience, you really know how undressed you can feel with an open coat. I suggested that we eat our lunch, and afterward I would take him to my tailor.

We went to the main dining room where Gene Cunningham, the assistant maitre'de, immediately knew he had two political candidates in custody and gave us the most prominent table by the door. All diners who entered passed within inches of our table, and many had the opportunity to meet Judge Smith and to wish us well on our campaign. After a healthy lunch, we drove to my tailor's, where it was his first time to serve either a judge or candidate.

I looked forward to Saturday evening as I had been "sold" two tickets to a meeting of the Polish American Century Club in Hamtramck, where Governor and Mrs. Romney were to be the principal guests. I asked one of my lady friends to accompany me — one of the most beautiful girls that I have ever met, with a figure to go with her face.

We arrived early as had been my policy during this campaign, and entered a spacious room filled with tables. Having gathered the insight into counting one's "customers" as soon as I entered a political arena, I discovered that they expected about three hundred for dinner.

This lady and I started off into a little bar off the main room, and found that the happy politicians were there. We pushed toward the bar, but never did reach it. Some distinguished-looking gentlemen entered the room, and I introduced myself. Immediately we were long-standing friends. When Governor and Mrs. Romney arrived, I had a few seconds to introduce them to my lady friend, and then the lining up and procession to the speakers' table began. I found that a gentleman of Polish descent was to be the toastmaster. He had difficulty pronouncing my name. I am sure that I could not have done as well with his name, which was Piotrowski.

After Mrs. Romney and I had both been introduced, next on the program was a young lady whom I believe was probably born in Poland, who was to sing for us. She sang one song, and before the toastmaster could begin his introduction of the governor, she sang another. Ultimately, at about the fifth song, he interrupted and that was the end of the singing. (The next week, as I sat by the governor on a high-school stage listening to a band play, I whispered to Mr. Romney that I understood the girl from Hamtramck was next on the program. He laughed heartily.)

It was then the governor's turn to speak. He presented flags to the heads of two Polish organizations which were active with war veterans. It was so humorous to hear him stumble on the difficult names. I recall that it took him four attempts to get a facsimile of the correct pronunciation. He again gave one of his outstanding speeches, without too much reference to politics.

As my friend and I left our table and talked with many friendly, smiley-faced people, we knew that association with this group would bring me many, many votes. Again, I realized the value of a beautiful girl to a politician.

Finally, it was the last week of my campaign. In one week the voters would be marking their ballots. I had to make this last week count.

I had been invited by the Economic Club of Detroit to a lunch where Governor Romney would speak. The affair would take place in the beautiful new Cobo Hall. Upon entering, I saw well over one hundred people. On inquiry, I was told that these were all the honored guests, and that the luncheon crowd would probably be near three thousand.

In our guest room, I moved around and soon found myself in a group with Dr. Harlan Hatcher, president of the University of Michigan, Dr. John Hanna, president of Michigan State University, and Dr. Clarence Hilberry, president of Wayne State University. The next moment I was shaking hands with the president of Chrysler Corporation, the president of Michigan Bell Telephone, and so it went. I knew that I was among the leaders of Michigan. When they called our names to be seated, I found myself directly in front of the governor. There were three other Republican candidates for state office present, and we were introduced by the head of the Economic Club.

Several times during his speech Governor Romney referred to me and to the other candidates, requesting that his team be elected. At the end of this meeting, I truly knew that I had been part of a great moment in history.

I returned to my office for the rest of the day, then home for dinner. Molly, our housekeeper, turned out to be a diligent worker on my behalf, distributing flyers and stickers. That afternoon we talked and I learned that she had personally asked over two hundred people to vote for me. I knew that Marie had done the same, and it made me feel warm all over to know that I had such loyal help.

The next day's schedule included eleven stops, the first in Grand Rapids at eight thirty in the morning. I had always liked my bed at home and hated to leave it, so I decided to get up at four thirty to make the nearly two-hundred-mile drive. When the alarm went off, I remembered my early morning trip to Kalamazoo, and my first move was to start the coffee percolating. As I drove through the miserable wet morning, I passed one of my fellow candidates, Bill Cudlip, who was heading for the same rendezvous. We soon found ourselves drinking coffee and talking to reporters.

One of the TV cameramen got the idea that we should be walking in the rain to show we were politicians who could not be daunted by rain, snow, or sleet. We found out that this is a fine way to take the crease out of a pair of pants, the press out of a coat, and to generally make you feel untidy for the rest of the day. But it did give us good publicity.

My lunch assignment was a Rotary meeting. The principal speaker turned out to be a lumber-and-building supply wholesaler. I knew this would be a profitable day. I could sell him some of my aluminium doors, siding, and other products. After lunch I talked him into taking me to his lumberyard.

Later, I went out with Mr. Cudlip to one of the beautiful banks where we were welcomed by the president, a long-standing friend of my fellow candidate. One next stop was to visit Paul Goebel, the former Mayor of Grand Rapids, who was also a former Michigan football hero. We spent some time in his office looking over his college trophies.

It was at Mr. Goebel's suggestion that we went to the newspaper to visit the editor. Mr. Woodruff was glad that we had stopped. In fact, he told us that our Democratic counterparts had visited him very recently, and that he was always happy to talk with candidates. After we left his office, I felt that I had not been as aggressive as I could have been. However, several days later I learned that Mr. Woodruff had come out supporting my candidacy.

I realized — and only too late in the campaign — that I should have been calling on the editors of papers regularly. (In fact only the day before, at the Economic Club luncheon, I had met the editor of the Detroit News and had made an appointment with him.)

Mr. Goebel then took Mr. Cudlip and me to his home, as we had a few minutes before our evening meeting. It was mighty nice to be welcomed by his lovely wife and to have an opportunity to shave before dinner. I arrived home at 2:30 A.M., after a good, full, twenty-two hours of continual on the foot and on the pedestal campaigning.

I had driven home late the night before because I had been invited by the president of the Detroit Rotary Club to be an honored member at the Wednesday lunch. My secretary, Muriel, came along and placed a piece of my literature at each of the several hundred luncheon plates. From the applause after my introduction, I was sure that I would get a lot of support from this group.

I had then scheduled myself to go to the *Detroit Free Press* for an interview with the political writers. My interrogator was very interested in talking with me, and we visited at great length about philosophies of education and the future. Then I went to the *Detroit News*. I learned that the editor and I were neighbors and his children were contemporaries of mine. I wish that I had visited both papers earlier in the campaign, having been told by both that my opponents had talked with them on several occasions. I do not know whether the outcome of my election would have been any different, but both papers had endorsed my opponent. I cannot say if I would have gotten more consideration had I visited earlier. My advice to any politician would be to cover the newspapers first, fast, and with real determination.

Thursday was another of those ten-event days. We would start off by visiting the Republican headquarters of several Detroit-area districts. In each, we were welcomed by supporters with coffee and donuts. It was an opportunity for us candidates to say "thank you" to a lot of loyal people who had worked hard for us.

We then went to lunch at a very nice restaurant where we were the guests of seventy-five elegant women. I was in good spirits, as I should have been, seated at a table with seven lovely women during the meal. We were then on to the first of three coffee stops with Judge Smith, where the ladies teased me about driving a Cadillac. This was a happy crowd and I'm sure the judge and I would have liked to spend the afternoon...However, duty called.

By the time we reached our second stop, hordes of children were also arriving. We immediately concluded that it was better to go coffee breaking and hand shaking when the kids were still in school. Our last gathering was in a neighborhood of elite homes with mature ladies who had evidently not wanted for any material things. They were cultured and we enjoyed talking with them.

I had made arrangements to have my Ann meet us for dinner and the evening. So, we set out within a half hour for the Dearborn Inn, our meeting place. All of the candidates were due there, as well as Governor Romney. However, the weather was the best that day of any during the campaign, and the governor had decided to stomp door-to-door on a street called Lenore (also his wife's name). So, without the governor we had a lovely dinner still, and Ann enjoyed every minute.

Next, we were off to Riverside High School for a press conference. As we entered, Governor Romney was speaking to a group of reporters. He paused in his speech and introduced me as the Wayne State candidate, and Ann as my beautiful daughter. This was Ann's first experience sitting in on a press conference, and she was proud to have the governor join us. In fact, Ann was very enthusiastic, and had decided that her father probably would be quite a politician after all.

The motif at the Riverside High rally was flying high some rather large kites — each candidate's banner. My little Nancy had been wild about kites, so Ann asked for a couple of them to take home. By the next afternoon those banners were again flying high — over Nancy's second-grade playground.

Friday passed like a fast ride across town. The morning began with a meeting of campaign workers prior to a mid-morning coffee with mostly retirees. At lunch we were the guests of a Republican women's group — six candidates and two hundred women. Our next meeting was with about sixty retired African-Americans. I realized that many had backgrounds in farming, so I talked about my experiences milking cows and driving horses, before moving on to our great public school system.

I was sure that I had done the best job of all my fellow candidates before this group. After another community meeting in Hamtramck, we were off to work the main gates at Dodge as the shift changed. The entrances and exits of large factories had only been hearsay to me prior to this time, and I must admit I imagined them with picketing and even violence. I was surprised. As the whistle blew, thousands of people passed by. I was amazed at how many hands reached out for my literature. I tried to say "thank you" to each as the cards slipped from my fingers.

Our evening appearance was with Governor Romney at the Cinderella Theater on the east side of Detroit. My telephone had buzzed with calls from friends about this event, and I dreaded it because it was so close to my Grosse Pointe Farms home. I knew that many friends and acquaintances would attend, possibly more from curiosity than a desire to help the party.

As I arrived alone, I was happy to be greeted by some old friends who had come to pass out my literature. I headed to the balcony where the governor was meeting with reporters. From there I could see the lobby where my friends were in the front line, handing out my cards and promoting my candidacy. I could not have arranged better coverage, or better friends, had I tried.

When my wife passed away, the experience with friends was similar. It was enlightening to see who stepped forward with a helping hand, and to wake to the realization that many of your supposed friends never lifted a hand or raised a voice to help in your time of need.

As we candidates marched down the aisle, the movie (we were in a theater) ground to a slow, screeching stop. As we climbed up to the stage, the governor pushed me forward and I became the first to face the lights. It was eerie sitting in the floodlights with the audience in the darkened room. Soon it was time for my five minutes, and I began to speak to the crowd of nine hundred. Somewhere along in the early part of my speech, a big man in the front row started saying "A-A-A-Amen." I would say another few words and he would call out his "A-A-A-Amen" again. The audience was catching the humor, and it appeared to me that this fellow may have visited one of the local bars before attending the meeting. The fellow probably imagined himself in church, with me as the minister. The long "A-A-A-Amen" continued throughout my speech. At the conclusion, I also ended with "A-A-A-Amen," which evoked hearty applause. I never did find out what happened to this fellow, and I never heard another "Amen" throughout the rest of the speeches.

When I arrived home, I mixed myself a martini, added six anchovy olives, and realized that I had had a very full day.

Saturday, the last working day before Monday's election, was a blank slate for me. Most of my fellow candidates had heavy weekend schedules in their home areas. However, I had accepted an invitation from my long-standing friend, Richard Durant, leader of the Republican Party in the Fourteenth District, to be his guest that evening. My mind went back some ten years to my first and only encounter with political life. It happened that Dick Durant was running for office, and my next door neighbor asked me to help campaign. Every evening my neighbor, Randy Babcock, and I would cover a street passing out Dick's literature and asking people to vote for him. Now I was his guest, with several other prominent Republicans, on the stage at Detroit's Denby High School.

Either I was tired from the six-week campaign, or anxious to continue the evening with my date, but I had a great deal of trouble keeping my mind on the comments. Afterwards, we invited several friends over for cocktails, and then my guests headed home.

Sunday was a day of rest, and on Monday morning I voted on my way to work. I had headed for my office expecting a good day of catchup. However, the telephone kept ringing with friends wishing me well. As I went through my factory, workers right and left kept saying, "I voted for you." Touring the office, I got the same reception. It was nice to be back at work.

At noon I slipped away to lunch, and the hostess at the restaurant told me that she had heard I was leading in the election. That was followed by several afternoon phone calls with the same news. That evening after dinner the phone rang again, and a friend who had listened to the radio all day informed me that I had slipped to a losing position. Some friends came to spend the evening with my children and me, eventually returning home when there were few reports on the tabulation of votes. At midnight, Ann went to bed. I watched television until 3:00 A.M., finally shutting it off.

In the morning I was awakened by little Nancy long before seven o'clock telling me that she had heard on television that I had 754,000 votes. We all got up at this early hour, and sure enough, that was my vote count. It was obvious that I had lost the election by a few votes, and that Leonard Woodcock was the victor with the second position a toss-up between Dr. Whitaker and the other Democratic opponent. At noon I learned from Dr. Whitaker that the *Detroit News* had called and told him he was "in." By evening the final tally was out, and I had come within twenty-one thousand votes of winning.

For all practical purposes, that was the end of my entree into politics, and I was ready to settle back to a normal life of earning a living.

I guess the spirit of politics is hard to drop. During the busy weeks of campaigning we candidates had often discussed a post-election party. I picked up the phone and called Art Elliott, and refreshed his memory on the party. He agreed it would be enjoyed by all the candidates as well as by the other Republican leaders. The governor's schedule was open on April 19, and so we began planning.

Once again, I was in new territory and felt weighed down with the burden of choosing a party site, menu, seating arrangements, flowers, etc. Talking with my number-one daughter, we decided to begin with a cocktail party at our home, and then go on to dinner at the Detroit Athletic Club.

As we surveyed the house, we determined that Nancy's battered baby table and chairs must go, and that we needed to order new guest towels, and a coffee table to replace Nancy's furniture.

I then went down to the Athletic Club to determine the menu and seating. The dinner was no problem. One thing I was sure of was that it should not include chicken or peas. I had had seventeen chicken dishes over the last weeks of campaigning. We ended up with filet.

There was a drawn-out discussion about seating. Does the governor sit at one end of the table and his lady at the other? It was concluded that they should both sit in the middle, across from one another. We worked everyone else in from that point, and it was a long, arduous process involving both Ann and my date for the evening, Lois.

In the early stages of planning I had asked Ann to be the party hostess, and, of course, this meant sitting next to the governor. Ann told me that she didn't really want that responsibility and would sooner be a carefree guest. So I called on my lady friend, Lois, who agreed to take the party on.

As the first guests arrived, I could tell that it was going to be a lively party. Since all of our male guests were involved in politics, you could be sure there would not be a lack of conversation. In fact, the cocktail party went so well that we were all a half hour late in leaving for the restaurant.

The evening went fast. Before we knew it, it was eleven o'clock and the Romneys decided to leave. Lois and I escorted them down the elevator and to their car. The first thing that Lois said as the Romneys drove off was to look at the dirt mark on the top of her shoe. She was obviously delighted at having been stepped on. The mark had been made by the governor when his first step in their dance was on her toe. She said she was going to frame that shoe and keep it for posterity. We returned to the party and the footprint was a source of lively conversation for the remainder of the evening.

And so went my political career.

Business as Usual

MY MEMBERSHIP IN THE YOUNG PRESIDENTS ORGANIZATION (YPO), AND then my subsequent belonging to the follow-up Chief Executives Organization (CEO), have been outstanding experiences in my lifetime. I had been involved in starting the Michigan chapter of YPO in 1953 when we had to find twelve members eligible to qualify for chapter status. I enjoyed twelve years with YPO, even though this was the period during which my Harriet contracted the cancer. With five years of illness, and another five years as a single parent, I did not have much time to enjoy all the activities of the group, including travel.

I probably had fifty friends who were in this group. I often felt that maybe their friendship derived from sympathy due to my family situation. With all of my responsibilities, I had to forego the honor of Chapter Chairman, even though I was pushed by several members to take the job and they would do the work. However, I did become fairly well known nationally in the YPO.

What I missed in quantity I made up in quality, because I was chosen to chair the first day of the 1963 International YPO convention in Hawaii. Governor and Mrs. Romney both accepted my invitation to be my speakers.

I went to Hawaii about two days prior to the opening of the convention to be sure everything was in order for the governor's speech. Almost immediately I was confronted with two similar problems. A representative from the Spanish-speaking contingent approached me with the fact that there were about fifty Spanish-speaking members present who wanted to hear the governor's message, but were afraid they wouldn't be able to interpret fast enough. About the same time, a representative of the German-speaking contingent approached me with the same problem. His group had about twenty-five members.

I was frantic as I did not know what to do. I presented the problem to the hotel manager. He solved it. The Spanish group would sit in one balcony, and the German group in the other balcony, each with earphones and an interpreter. Was I happy and relieved!

The day arrived — my introduction of Lenore Romney first, and then Governor Romney.

Now, this was an election year, and at the time of the conference Governor Romney was a strong contender for the Republican presidential nomination. One of his opponents was Nelson (Rocky) Rockefeller of New York. I laced my introduction heavily with this contest as there were many New Yorkers present. My final sentence was "Governor Romney will have many a Rocky Road to travel." In both Spanish and German this inclusion of "Rocky" must have had a special meaning, as both groups gave the comment a standing ovation.

At the end of the governor's speech, he asked me to call the governor of Hawaii for him, as he felt it was his duty to let the Hawaiian governor know that he was in Hawaiian territory. So it was that I found myself in the company of two governors for the rest of the day, as I was invited along to tour the main Hawaiian island. I realized that there are only fifty governors in the whole United States, and I was spending the day with two of them.

At your fiftieth birthday you are automatically out of the YPO. There are two follow-up organizations, and I was offered membership in the Chief Executives and accepted.

Two years before my tenure with YPO ran out, three fellow members asked me to serve on their companies' Boards of Directors, and I accepted. The largest of these was the Sparton Corporation in Jackson, Michigan. This was a great honor, and a great follow-up to my Republican political career.

In 1963, when I first had the privilege of becoming a Director of Sparton Corporation, a large part of their business was in music. At that time the company was seventy years old, and had been a pioneer in manufacturing the original, crank-type phonographs. I particularly remember the promotion of a hound sitting in front of a large horn, with the caption "His Master's Voice."

My first out-of-state trip as a Sparton Corporation director was to one of their factories in London, Ontario, where ten and twelve inch phonograph disc records were stamped out. There were probably twenty machines, and each time a plate came down, another record was produced. On this particular day, they were stamping Beethoven's Fifth Symphony.

Everyone knows what happened to disc phonograph records, and accordingly, they went by the wayside in the Sparton operation.

In place of records, Sparton developed a line of sonobuoys for and with the U.S. Navy. Sonobuoys are underwater detection devices which are planted in the seas, usually around a port, to detect enemy submarines.

In the early sixties, President Kennedy was having his problems with the Russian government relative to the Cuban missile crisis. At this time, we were told that the Sparton sonobuoys completely surrounded the island of Cuba to detect the entry of Russian subs.

In addition to sonobuoys, Sparton developed many lines of other high-tech products, including a line of parts for the automobile industry developed by company president John J. Smith. One of the chief items were the horns which were installed on many of our leading automobiles.

In 1965 I read in the Sunday paper that cities would soon be joined together to form megalopolises as our population grew. This article stated that Ann Arbor, Toledo, and Detroit would merge into a megalopolis, with the center being known as Garden City (which was unincorporated at that time). I thought that if I bought land in Garden City, I could sell it off and become a mega-millionaire. I found a pasture dotted with horses from a riding stable. I bought the land. This is where my business would grow to three plants that would manufacture products that I had not yet dreamed of.

F o u r t e e n

Meeting Sandra

IN THE SPRING OF 1964 CHIP GRADUATED FROM DARTMOUTH. I TOOK MY
three little children, Ann, Bill, and Nancy, and my nephew, Erling
Noecker, from North Dakota, to the graduation. On the first day we
drove approximately seven hundred miles, deciding to stop in
Burlington, Vermont at a motel, as the kids were tired. We checked in
at about 11:00 P.M., after stopping on our way to view Niagara Falls.

At about 6:00 A.M., big air hammers and road equipment started
pounding in the parking lot, probably not more than thirty feet from our
window. It woke us, and I called down to the office and complained bit-
terly about stopping for a good night's sleep and then being awakened
so early in the morning. My complaint produced no results, so I kept
calling. Suddenly, there was a knock at the door, and upon opening it,
saw a man who said he was the manager.

I should have been the guy who was mad, but he was angry at me for complaining. He said, "You people from the Midwest feel that you can come into our New England territory and boss us around." After heated words, he pulled back his fist as though he was going to hit me, and I said, "I have a son and a nephew over in that bed who are both about six foot six, and if you touch me, you will never walk down those stairs again." With that remark I heard the biggest pair of snickers from under the covers that any father has ever heard. The boys laughed as we got the girls out of bed and dressed, and left the motel at a very early hour.

The biggest joke came ten miles down the road when I realized that I'd forgotten my pajamas in the room. The kids rationalized that the motel manager would have stuffed them with Vermont hay, hanged me in effigy, and set fire to the body swinging from the rope. They were so sure that's what happened to my pajamas that the story has been told and retold as a family joke.

On graduation day the weather was beautiful, and after the program the Dartmouth College presented each graduate with a family luncheon. Our table, outside under the trees, consisted of me with the five children. All around us there were tables of ten, fifteen, and twenty people, each supporting their graduate. I realized at this time how important family support is, and made up my mind to develop blood relatives into a supportive family group.

After the graduation ceremony we planned to drive into New York City to attend the World's Fair. Chip had a Plymouth convertible at school, and we drove two cars to Albany, New York, where we left his car in a motel parking lot before driving into New York City.

On the first evening we went to a play, whose star was a young lady by the name of Teresa Brewer, whose hometown was Toledo, Ohio. I can't remember the name of the play, but I do recall that she was the star for our group.

The next morning we went to the World's Fair. As we embarked on our day's adventure, my nephew, Ehrling, who was probably fifteen at the time, announced that he would meet us at the exit at 4:00 P.M. I couldn't imagine that my little nephew from North Dakota, who had never seen a big city, would be so at home as to tell me he would meet me five hours later. Somehow, I had to say okay, and we set out in different directions. But all day long I worried about him.

That evening we went to a play that starred Carol Burnett. I can't remember the title, but the plot included a lady that died, her husband who remarried, and her ghost which appeared every day. In 1964, both Teresa Brewer and Carol Burnett were undiscovered stars.

Another notable memory of this trip is that we stayed at the Hotel Pierre, which was where Herbert Hoover had a room for many years while he was the president. I received the reservation through one of the vice presidents at Reynolds Aluminum, and when I wrote to confirm, I jokingly asked the manager if we could sleep in President Herbert Hoover's room. To my surprise, when we arrived at the hotel, President Hoover's room had been reserved for us. So, Ann and Nancy slept in Herbert Hoover's bed for three nights while we were in New York City.

This period of my life was highlighted by being both mother and father to my four young children. Yet I had time to meet quite a few young ladies who were interesting to me, and I to them. I had my rules that I followed: no girlfriend under twenty-four or over thirty-six; no paying someone's way to a distant city or convention. And I limited my children's exposure to my girlfriends. With these guidelines, and a few others which are not necessary to mention, I existed for four-and-a-half years as a relatively happy, single man. I had concluded that if a person keeps his body clean, dresses up to the minute, sits on a reasonably large billfold, is over six foot tall, and is reasonably good looking, with hair or without, he can do quite well socially.

I had enjoyed a wonderful marriage of nineteen years with Harriet, and, I'm sure, like many men in similar situations, I thought I would never marry again. For five years I cared for her when she was ill. For five years I had been a single parent raising four children.

On September 3, 1965, I first met my Sandra.

Of my many manufacturing storm-window dealers across the country, I had one very outstanding lady who ran a business in our backyard — Wyandotte, Michigan. She was outstanding as a business person, sales person, and she represented the best in social graces. Over the years she mentioned her children to me, and one day in 1965 she asked me to introduce her divorced daughter to some of my single friends in the YPO and business world. I agreed.

A young hotel entrepreneur and I were planning a social evening, and I happened to think of my dealer's request. I remember calling her home, telling her that I was going to dinner at the "Top of the Flame" and then on to the Fisher Theater, and I wondered if her daughter might be interested in going with me. As I waited on the telephone, I heard her say, "This is Marshall Noecker, and he's going to invite you out for an evening, and by God, you'd better go."

Sandra met me at the "Top of the Flame" and I'll always remember the feeling within my brain, and my body, when she stepped from the elevator on the twenty-second floor. I was amazed.

After dinner we drove to the Fisher Theater. Normally, I would have enjoyed the performance, but my mind was otherwise absorbed. As we walked down the long lobby our hands found one another. Nothing had ever felt like this before. I couldn't believe it was happening to me. All of the rest of the world was lost. In two hours, I was in love!

Our seats were in Row M, in the middle section. I should have been facing the stage, but I'm sure my head and neck had assumed a ninety-degree turn to the right. I'm glad to have been able to turn my head back to the normal position.

At the end of the performance we got in my car and drove back downtown where her car was parked. At that hour it was the only car left in the lot. We got out, I unlocked her car door, and after just a moment's hesitation, our arms and bodies locked together. A normal hug and kiss is just a perfunctory feeling. But this was different. Later, I found out she felt the same tingle that I did.

After that evening I thought "to hell with introducing her to other young men, as she was made for me and me for her." But, to satisfy her mother, I did introduce her to a restaurant entrepreneur who was very short, very heavyset, and too old for her.

For those of you who have fallen deeply in love, you can think of nothing but the person of your affections. That was my situation. Sandra was living with her parents, and as sometimes happens, everything seemed to fall in place.

After our first date, Sandra's parents were away in Europe for a six-weeks business and vacation trip, and "when the cat's away, the mice will play." Her parents lived in a beautiful home with a swimming pool. In the pool area was a dressing and play room which had a lighted ceiling. By lighted, I mean the heavens were shown twinkling stars highlighted by the Little and Big Dippers. Now, to truly view this phenomenon of the sky, the best method was to lie on your back, looking at the ceiling. Therefore, we found ourselves in that position, watching the heavens. I think that these factors all contributed to hasten matrimony.

Throughout September, Sandra and I were engaged in a very, very social program which through to our December wedding included: a kiss in the parking lot of the University Club; dinner at my home to meet Nancy and Bill; dinner at Sandra's home and relaxing on davenport until 5:00 A.M.; dinner, and first dancing, at Detroit Athletic Club; a formal party at the Detroit Golf Club, where I asked Sandra to marry me; then church, and dinner at my home, where Sandra said, "yes."

Within a few weeks of our meeting, I had "popped the question." I promised her two baby daughters in addition to marriage. I am not sure whether this sewed up the deal, but I think it helped.

Sandra had two little boys, six and nine years old, and I had four children. We decided that we could handle the situation, as well as the two little girls that I promised her.

When Sandra's parents arrived home from Europe, she told them of our plans to marry. Sandra's mother was absolutely flabbergasted to think that her daughter would marry an older man with four children, and she went to bed for a week.

While in bed, she decided to find out what her daughter was getting into, and ordered a Dunn and Bradstreet report on me. Since I have always kept my financial and business matters personal, the amount of information she received was minimal. I had told Sandra that "I really wasn't that tall, I was just sitting on my billfold." I would like to report that after the week in bed, her mother recovered with great enthusiasm and presented us with several of the nicest engagement parties, and the greatest wedding, that anyone could enjoy.

So, we tied the knot on December 28, and went off on a three-day honeymoon, returning New Year's Day. We picked up Sandra's two sons before facing my contingent of four. I can tell you that it was quite an experience to come home from your honeymoon and to put two little strangers to bed in a home with four other children. This was not a simple task, and also not a situation that many newly-wedded people have to confront. Somehow, we managed.

When Sandra said, "I do," it was a decision made by the two of us.

The children had little to say about joining families, but there were no objections, at least known to us. In the first ten months of our marriage, all of our time and energy were absorbed as parents.

I realized that I had found the perfect mate. Sandra was always on time. She was always perfectly groomed and beautifully dressed. Meals were always on time, and they were adequate to delicious. In a family this size, there is never enough money to cover all the needs, but somehow Sandra made it "go around" and I never felt pressure to "bring home more bacon." Wealth was growing, but in businesses and not in expendable cash.

Comments from my friends were always, "Where did you find this girl?"

Sandra's attitude was always directed to the good of every family member. She realized that the financial success of a family leads to benefits for every member. She listened to me, night after night, tell what I had accomplished that day, and what my goals for the future embodied. We entered into discussion, but rarely an argument, on my procedures. Her comments were always, "I have great faith in you." How can a husband but be successful with the support of a wife like this?

Only a few days after our families merged, we took Sandra's son, Rick, to the third grade, and Greg to the first grade, in their new school, where my Nancy was a fourth grader. Bill was in the large high school, while Ann was a sophomore at the University of Michigan, and Chip was a young C.P.A. working in New York City.

On the first day of school, Sandra received a telephone call stating that Bill was sick at the high school from something he had eaten in the cafeteria, and his mother was to come and pick him up. This was a funny situation as Sandra had no idea what the name of the school was or where it was located. She stumbled around with the nurse, saying that she did not know the name of the school or its location, and the nurse was flabbergasted that a mother would not know where her child was going to school, its name, or location. Many times Sandra has told this story of how she lacked words in explaining to the nurse that she was a newly-married mother and had never heard of Bill's school. We experienced many similar situations in the next few months, and probably the most disconcerting to Sandra, and also to me, were the girls that I had known that would call my home for me, and when they would ask whom they were talking to, Sandra would say, "Mrs. Noecker." Then the receivers would click, or the inquisition would begin. But, we lived through it all.

One wintry day Sandra, Nancy, Greg, Rick, and I were on our way to the airport when Greg announced that he had to go to the bathroom. Right away. I stopped the car, jumped out, took him by the hand and led him about twenty feet up the steep slope on the fringe of the expressway. The wind was blowing from the south. Greg lined himself up to do his duty, also facing south. You can imagine what happened. His clothes were getting sprinkled. Standing halfway down the slope, I yelled at him to turn around. He did not understand me, so I ran up the slope, grabbed him by the shoulder, and turned him north.

This has become a saying in our family — that when doing your duty you should always know from which direction the wind is blowing.

In October of 1966 Sandra and I realized we were embarking on our first trip as husband and wife as we headed to Eastern Canada for five days at a Chief Executives Convention.

Of course, we had had a three-day honeymoon, but a honeymoon is a honeymoon, and no one thinks of responsibilities.

As we rolled along, we talked about our life together — what it would be like and where it would lead us. To be successful in my business life, Sandra knew she would have to give me plenty of freedom to make business decisions, many that would be at a sacrifice to her and the children. So often when the husband is tending to his daily business affairs, situations develop where he has to plan trips on the spur of the moment. He cannot come home and have his wife be unhappy with his decision, or second guess him. Sandra understood this point, and it was probably on this first trip that she assured me to "forge ahead."

On the other hand I knew she had the same decision-making responsibilities running the home and guiding the children. I would do no second guessing. We both wanted our marriage to be happy and successful.

In every marriage there are times when tempers flair and get out of hand. We decided our marriage was for the long haul, and tempers would be handled like a bump in the road. Just put our heads down and keep going.

Marriage counselors know that money problems are near the top of the list in causes of divorce. We would be no different. Money would raise its ugly head in our lives. We knew that education would swallow up a lot of money from kindergarten on, as we had children who had a thirst for learning. After young Marshall chose Dartmouth, we knew a pattern had been set. They all wanted the best colleges and universities. And we received no financial aid. I made ten cents an hour too much. We also knew that when a man has his own businesses, the family income is not always the same year after year. Some years we would eat steak, and some we would have macaroni and cheese. We knew we had to "roll with the tide." All of my extra money went into businesses. At one time, I had seventeen corporations in six different fields of business.

A few years after our marriage, my housekeeper of many years, Marie, died. In most families, the household would have faced a calamity. At this time we had seven children in our home — three of my four older ones, Sandra's two boys, and our babies, Nicholas, two years old, and Alexandra, just a few months. Sandra realized it was impossible to replace Marie, and so, she ran the home. She got the older children off to school, took care of the babies, and cooked the meals with a minimal amount of day help.

When Sandra and I were married, there was only one way to go for housing, and that was to move into the home which I'd enjoyed for the past ten years. The house was seventy-two feet in length, and we could have had a bowling alley in the basement, but we spent several thousand dollars fixing up a playroom for the children. Only we couldn't get the kids to play there for any reason!

Over the next ten years we accumulated architectural prints and designs for our "dream house." We had a pile approximately eight inches thick of torn-out magazine pages. We knew what we wanted after a decade of dreaming, and we found a lot that was an adequate size, was close to our choice of schools, and in a very nice, new neighborhood called Grosse Pointe Farms.

The house we built was fifty-four feet wide, and forty foot deep, with two stories — one exactly over the other. Sandra wanted to be able to watch the children's play from the kitchen, so the back half of the first floor was one large room. In the upstairs, we had four bedrooms and three baths, built for when the children were still at home, but with the time when they would come home with their own children also in mind.

Part of this house plan goes back to my childhood days when we would travel by sleigh to my Grandfather Noecker's home, with the two-foot wide windowsills. We built them into our sunroom, which we then furnished with the antique wicker furniture that Sandra inherited from her parents' estate when they passed away.

When we built our new home in 1976, I was making greenhouses in my Noecker Window and Door Corporation. We were selling and installing these units for quite a number of high-profile customers, particularly members of the Red Wings Hockey team and other athletic stars. I thought we had hit on another great market. So, in the area behind our large family room, we built a Noecker greenhouse — ten foot deep by twenty wide, equipped with a gas heater for winter, and hinged roof windows to vent the hot air out in the summer.

We grew tomatoes, peppers, cucumbers, and cabbages year round. Sandra was president of the Grosse Pointe Garden Club for two years, raising the most beautiful flowers you could imagine.

Our greenhouse was not without problems. Broken branches from our tall trees broke several glass roof panels, and God always seemed to make this happen in the coldest weather. Our gas heater did its job, until the temperature dipped below zero. Then we would resort to opening doors and fanning heat from the house into the greenhouse.

Ten years later, with most of the children in college or working, we decided we had had enough of tomatoes year round, and the greenhouse went. We built a sunroom in its place, with two skylights and Grandfather Noecker's wide windowsills — wide enough for future grandchildren to play and nap on.

Our garage was another story. Sandra remembered the stories of the Sears-catalog Saxons that Ray and I drove, and when she saw an ad in our local paper for a 1953 MG, we bought it. Bill, who was nearing his legal driving age, rode home with me in the MG.

We laid out our garage to hold four cars — two antiques and two current sized. Four units side by side would have made the garage look bigger than the house from the street, so we decided on two wide and two deep, just the way we strung our horses out for work on the farm.

From an economic standpoint, antique cars are a good investment. We have been told that there are only three 1953 MG — TF1500s like ours in the U.S. today, and that in the thirty-one years we've owned ours, it's increased thirty-eight times in value.

F i f t e e n

Extrusion Expansion

I BELIEVE THERE HAS NEVER BEEN A BETTER TIME IN THE BUSINESS WORLD than in the thirty years following World War II. It seemed that no one could make a mistake in business. To be successful, one had to choose a growing industry at the right time. And aluminum was the product I chose.

We started in the extrusion business in 1963 when I bought the Ferguson plant. The operation was on Mt. Elliott in Detroit for several years. At that time, the extrusion industry was pretty much in its infancy, for extruded windows, doors, and certainly the bus shelters we later built, had not yet appeared.

One of my first steps was to build on the Garden City land. It had been my thought to move both my storm window and door operations to that area to take advantage of potential growth. However, somewhere along the line I decided that the coming field was aluminum extrusions. An aluminum-extrusion machine operated similar to pushing toothpaste out of a container. A slug of alloyed aluminum is heated to about nine hundred degrees and pushed through a die which has the contour of the shape the customer requires. Since I had bought the Ferguson extrusion plant and operated it successfully for a couple years, I would move the press to that location. This was a little press which used a billet, or section of casting, and was just four inches in diameter, sixteen inches long, and weighing about fifteen pounds. All transferring of billets from the heating unit to the press was handled with hand tongs.

With our extruded-window program, we were able to convert all of our Canadian storm window manufacturers to extrusions. At the time, the Canadians were charging us a duty to send our extrusions into their country. This duty made us noncompetitive in the Canadian market. Therefore, to hold my manufacturing dealers I needed a good, reliable source of extrusions in Canada. I had two alternatives — to make arrangements with a Canadian extruder, or to buy an aluminum-extrusion company.

To my surprise, our people found a small extruder in Wallaceburg which we purchased. As often happens, in addition to a company which I needed, we also inherited a wonderful plant manager who worked for me for the rest of his life.

This company was located on a side street, and when we ran a long extrusion, we had a problem. Our yard was too short. I was able to get a permit from the city to close the street on those days when we ran extrusions that were longer than our yard. It was always interesting to see the street closed off with extrusions crossing it.

This company made us a factor in the Canadian extrusion industry. Our ad read "We are Canada's fifth largest aluminum extruder." My competitors turned this slogan around to read "Wallaceburg Aluminum is Canada's smallest aluminum extruder." Both statements were true.

In my travels around Canada to visit our manufacturing dealers, one winter I found myself in Winnipeg. My dealer there was a handsome, big, man, well built, strong, and sturdy. We had dinner at a nice restaurant, and when we left, the hatcheck girl held up a coat which she thought was mine. I slipped my arms and shoulders into it, and to my surprise, this coat must have weighed fifty pounds and the material seemed an inch thick. Even though I was born and raised three hundred miles south of Winnipeg, I had never felt that much weight in a coat.

I don't know why little things that happen in a person's life stay with him — but the weight of that coat comes to the forefront of my mind every time I think of Canada.

After operating the Canadian Wallaceburg plant for three years, we were approached by a company in Toronto who wanted to buy the press to manufacture a line of stair and carpet moldings and other fixtures. On a Saturday morning we met, and within a few hours had our cash and walked out of Canada's extrusion market with a smile on our faces. This was the second company that I had sold. The first was the aluminum chair business which financed our roll-form operations in the siding and awning industries. Our projects put a lot of young people through college. The rest we "hid" in Canada.

At around the same time we were also doing business in Nigeria with Eddy Adedeji, and received more than our due in publicity based on the volume of business we did with him.

First, the Bank of Africa decided to open a branch office in New York City, and I received an invitation from the prime minister of Nigeria to attend the ceremony. Not having many opportunities to float with international bankers, I accepted. On my arrival at the festivities in New York City, I discovered that more than half of the people were dressed in the ceremonial robes of their countries. Accordingly, I felt like a fish out of water, and said to the first man I was introduced to that I was unfamiliar with the customs of the African business communities. To my surprise he said, "Just call everybody a chief, and they will be very pleased and happy."

So, I spent the evening talking with a lot of chiefs. In addition, the prime minister of Nigeria invited me and my wife to Lagos to celebrate our business venture with Eddy Adedeji, and I accepted. However, about two weeks before our scheduled trip, I opened a copy of an international magazine and there was a photograph of the prime minister holding his hands up in the air. His premiership had just fallen to a coup. Our plans were canceled.

One order that Eddy Adedeji sold during the ten-year period that we did business was too large for him to manufacture, so we agreed to do it in Detroit. Naturally, we secured a letter of credit for the $350,000 job, payable through a New York bank.

To our surprise, the customer made arrangements for the windows to be shipped out of the port of New Orleans, while the invoice had to be certified by a company in Miami.

When it came time to ship the windows, we loaded seventeen large trucks in Detroit, which convoyed to New Orleans. I helped supervise the loading at the port, and then within minutes, was on a plane to Miami to secure release of the documents. That night I was again airborne, this time headed to New York City, where the bank released a check in payment in full.

During that same time period, our former governor, G. Mennen Williams, was appointed by President Kennedy to represent our country to the African nations. I read in the newspaper that Williams was going to be vacationing on Mackinac Island in northern Michigan, and so I jumped into my new Cadillac and headed north.

Governor Williams accepted my invitation for a conference, and I asked him to call on Eddy Adedeji in Nigeria. Some months later, I received a great letter of appreciation from Eddy, telling me that he had been visited by the governor. Some years later, I saw the governor and he told me that during his tenure in the African nations mine was the only request from an American businessman to call on an African associate. I considered this a surprise, and also a great achievement for me.

Our awning and siding business just kept growing and growing, and it was necessary for us to erect a new building to house the equipment. I built the same building off the same architectural plans three times in Garden City, twice in Detroit, and once in Southgate, as well as once in the United Kingdom — 44,000 square feet each.

The 1965 building paralleled my romance with Sandra — both began in September and produced great results in December.

Some time during the summer of 1965, I found that there was a 1,250 ton Watson Stillman extrusion press in mothballs in Jackson, Michigan. I made an offer, and Bob Yazejian used his engineering training to move the press from Jackson to Garden City. In addition, we engaged a young man by the name of Al Johnson to do the electrical work, and make the air and oil cylinders functional.

During this period Eddy Adedeji convinced Al to fly over and work on his factory in Nigeria, which he did. I was not in favor of this trip, and told Al he was completely on his own. After a few weeks in Lagos he came back with wonderful tales.

Six months later Eddy needed help again, and Al went. On arrival home Al was very sick and went into an Ann Arbor hospital where he was diagnoses with malaria. Within three days he was dead.

One of the programs that President Gerald Ford supported was public transportation. His director of this program suggested a competition for a bus shelter design. Up until this time shelters had been rather crude and flimsily built, with no design for convenience. I heard of this competition and thought of the aluminum domes that I had been making for skylights. I went to work with an engineer whom I had brought over from Europe, and we designed the shelter that presently can be seen across the country. The government liked my design using two domes, brackets for seats, with space for advertising and schedules.

The next thing we knew we were given a contract for a large quantity of bus shelters to be installed in Pontiac and Detroit. These contracts came at a time when we did not have a shelter, the extrusions, or a plant to build them in. It was similar to our three thousand jalousie window order from the Hawaiian hotel.

We rented a building in Garden City, close to my extrusion and paint plants, and before we were well into the first two contracts, had orders from Boston, Cleveland, Washington D.C., and other cities. Overnight we were a national manufacturer of a product that sold itself.

Not being content with the manufacture of extrusions and construction of bus shelters, we decided to get into making the domes. We found that plexiglass could be heated and formed into almost any desired shape. Soon manufacturers were coming from all over to observe our process.

I was a "nut" on securing patents for every little idea. I had been granted nearly eighteen patents, with over 147 patent features in the home-improvement industry. These include patents on windows, doors, awnings, window sashes, screens, and many variations on each.

I had made money on only one patent when I sold the rights to a large lumber company. The cash from this sale was sizeable, and I decided to set up a profit-sharing program for my employees at this time. So, I opened a profit-sharing account at one of our local banks and deposited this money into this profit-sharing program. I felt that this money really belonged to my employees as they helped me no end in setting in ideas, some of which were patentable. Therefore, it was their cash. In the last few years, I have had five employees retire and withdraw very sizeable funds from this program to make their lives easier in retirement.

As with most of our product lines, we did not stop on the first item with bus shelters. By the mid-seventies our country became conscious of the dangers of smoking. Companies were making their buildings off-limits to smokers, and you would see dozens of people light up outside of doors, in backyards, and anywhere else. Many companies realized that this was an inconvenience for valuable employees who also happened to be smokers.

I hit upon the idea of building smoking shelters. We put a door on our bus shelters and sealed the bottoms, and literally created a room with plexiglass sides for smokers.

From a promotional standpoint we got the idea of letting off smoke bombs in a shelter so that when smoke was pouring out the cracks, we could take a photograph. We had a great ad of our smoking shelter which brought us smiles, and most important, business.

By this time, I had my first two extrusion plants operating in Garden City and a growing market for painted aluminum extrusions. With our awning structures and storm windows and doors requiring paint, I had the idea that we had to get into the painting of extrusions.

My first step was building a paint plant in Garden City next to the extrusion plant. At this time there were no painting lines for lineal extrusions on the market, so we had to design our own system. We had seen automatic car-washing machines, where cars are attached to a chain in the floor and pulled past the washing equipment. Accordingly, we made our paint line powered by a floor chain, with movable cars hooked to the chain and pulled through the paint line. Some time later, we realized that we had to wash the extrusions, etch them with chemicals, and heat them so the paint would stick. I engineered tanks on overhead cranes to do the job. Made in 1972, twenty-five years later we could not see any room for improvement. To power the cranes we used a hoisting system powered by an electric motor operated through a Buick (car) transmission.

Our system was quite profitable until "do-gooders" got in the way and tried to control the amount of volatile organic compounds emissions (VOCs) that we could expel into the atmosphere, and the amount of chemicals that we could drain into the city water disposal system. During the first years there were no requirements on the solid waste, and we had no trouble disposing of it. However, as time went on, we ended up with problems that I hired a nice young man by the name of Dan Lingeman to help solve. Dan and I were summoned to Chicago for a meeting with the Environmental Protection Agency (EPA). We entered a room and were told to sit on one side of a table. On the other side were five young ladies, probably not over twenty-five years old, and one wilting young man. All were recent college graduates hired by the EPA. They harassed us on three problem areas, and after more trips to Chicago, they started telling us that we exceeded many of the allowed minimums and were subject to criminal action. After listening to the threats, my good man, Dan, my white hope for the paint industry, left me for other pastures. He said he could not sleep at night.

My son, Bill, had graduated from Cornell University, received his M.B.A. from the University of Michigan, his C.P.A. certificate from the State of Michigan, and had five years experience with one of the country's "Big Eight" accounting firms. Bill was now interested in the aluminum industry, and we decided to build another unit in Garden City.

We purchased an 1,800 ton Sutton extrusion press for slightly more than one million dollars. With the building and the press, we had slightly more than two million dollars invested in this program. Bill was appreciative, and rolled up his shirt sleeves as he went to work. He hired two college students for the summer of 1978, and the three of them completed the installation and were ready to produce. With our expanding volume, we soon kept this press running two shifts a day. It was time to sell the little, four-inch press that I had purchased in 1963.

I ended up making slightly more than twice what I paid for it. This definitely was a good time for business in America.

During that period I hired a die serviceman, a native from south of the border, which was not uncommon. He had quite a large family, and three of his sons were working for me in 1980 when we experienced our "Mexican Revolution."

A "friend" and long-standing competitor decided to go into the aluminum-extrusion business. He purchased an old press which had been left standing in a field near Belding, Michigan. Naturally, he needed manpower — experienced manpower — and my Mexican family looked good to him. They were good. The next thing I knew, all four of my Mexican crew walked out the door to work for my competitor who set up shop in Novi.

The aluminum-extrusion industry is very difficult to enter into, as it requires a heavy investment in machinery and equipment, and also needs experienced workers and technology. So, within three years, our competitor was experiencing difficulties. We watched for awhile, and when the proper time came, we made an offer. It was accepted, and we became a two-plant extrusion operation.

Our first action was to finish the Mexican Revolution. Even though we knew the father and two of the sons were very qualified employees, we had to make the break with them. Fortunately, I had a young college man — Dwight Fairchild — who had worked with me for about three years in Garden City. He transferred to Novi and took over.

Always being one to operate on the principle of never leaving a business enemy, I was able to engage the former competitor's sales operation to be my sales force for the "new" extrusion plant in Novi. From this sales group we inherited an energetic young man who had just become a C.P.A. He did a great job for us then, and is still one of our lead salesmen.

In the late eighties I learned that the General Motors Corporation had an extrusion operation — including the press and most of the allied equipment — for sale. This was a twenty-two hundred ton press with a capacity for a nine-inch billet, which was just exactly what we needed to compliment our two, six-inch presses, and a seven-inch machine. General Motors had turned this potential sale over to a young saleslady. I inspected the press, and realized that it would cost a lot of money to move it. Additionally, we learned that General Motors wanted the press moved in hurry because they needed the space to assemble pick-up trucks which were selling quite well. So, we put in a rather low bid. To our surprise, in one week's time we were the owners of our fourth extrusion press.

This was before Dan Lingeman's departure, and I put him in charge of moving this press. First it was loaded on trucks and sent to Ohio to be modernized. Within four months the pits for the press installation were dug, the reinforcements were in the floor, and press was reworked and installed.

In connection with this purchase, we secured quite a few items from General Motors, used in their program, that we did not need. Dan sold off the surplus, and surprisingly, his sales almost equaled our purchase price of two million dollars. We had our biggest press in operation for a small cash outlay.

To replace Dan Lingeman at our paint plant, I found a young man, a college graduate, to fit our needs. He ran the plant successfully for about three years, and then the Ford Motor Company raided us and offered our second white hope more money than we could afford to pay him. I was disappointed to lose him, but have always been supportive when an employee is able to, at least in his mind, better himself. This was a single young man with a good girlfriend whom he married while in our employ.

This was not to be the only news at the paint plant. On June 10, 1993 (my birthday), I had just shared a large lunch hosted by Dave Padilla, Bob Smith, and Bob Yazejian, and we were all happily sitting in my office when my phone rang. Our paint plant was on fire!

I jumped in my car and drove the thirty miles to Garden City as fast as I could. By the time I arrived, the fire department had doused the flames, and we watched the smoke billow from the water-soaked paint.

We were just at the beginning of our busy summer season, but were fortunate to line up two competitors to paint materials for us. We did have to haul the extrusions twenty miles to Novi, or two hundred to Ohio.

Our plant was fully insured, and after again pulling out the original architectural drawings, our builder promised completion of the plant structure in six weeks.

We also received a check for inventory, machinery, and equipment, and had to decide whether to reconstruct with a liquid paint line, or switch to powder coat which was a new field. After consulting the equipment manufacturers, we decided on the powder coat.

After twenty years — from 1972 to 1993 — in the aluminum-extrusion painting business, I felt that right or wrong, I knew as much about machinery, equipment, painting, layout, and the rest of the business as anyone in the country. Therefore, I decided to be my own layout man, engineer, electrician, and general supervisor of the paint plant.

I started with the overhead crane system, increasing the two loading areas to five. This meant that our system could handle thirty-six load bars prepared and ready to go through the paint booth and aging ovens before being packed for shipment.

In our old system we had ninety continuous feet of drying oven space to cure the paint. I got the idea to run the racks into the new, larger oven, and then direct the system to carry them sideways and out the other end. By loading sideways, we were able to utilize over seven hundred foot of oven. To my knowledge, no one else in the country has an aging capacity like this. And it is all controlled by computers. Aren't they wonderful? Our new paint line also used less gas, as we were able to operate it at a lower temperature for a great savings.

The dip tanks were not damaged by the fire, but the contents had to be replaced since the roof above them was completely demolished, as well as the overall crane system for dipping the racks of extrusions into the tanks. We also had two paint booths — one dedicated to white paint only. Since we need dozens of colors to satisfy the market, the second booth is for colors. Only one is used at a time, with a technician controlling the thickness of the powder coat on the bottom and top sections of each load bar. The color booth is not as efficient as the white booth. We purchased eight tanks where we stored the seven most popular colors, leaving one for miscellaneous colors. To change from one color to another in one of the main booths, it takes approximately four hours for two men to clear out the tanks, pipes, and nozzles. By having the second paint booth with the seven tanks containing specific colors it was not necessary to clean out any of the tubes and nozzles as they are changed with the insertion of the required tank. The eighth tank is completely changed as it supplies the various different colors.

To wind up our improvements and increased capacity, we had to have the capability of packing the materials. One of our leaders, Dwight Fairchild, and I engineered a circular wrapping machine and had to have it custom made. We found an engineering company in Lansing who built us a fine machine capable of wrapping bundles up to thirty-two feet long.

It is interesting to note that we had all of these projects working at one time. Richard-Wilcox on the overhead crane, Nordson of Cleveland on the two paint booths, Belco in Grand Rapids on the aging oven, Larson Engineering on the overhead crane over the dip tanks, and the company in Lansing making the wrapping equipment.

So, in only seven months, we had engineered and constructed what we considered to be the most outstanding paint plant in the country. When we reopened on January 18, 1994 our equipment could handle three times the paint volume of our previous system, so that we could grow with the industry.

With the new process in place, I had a story to tell customers. If business ever really got tough, Sandra and I could come in one day, load the thirty-six load bars, come in the second day, and run them through the paint booth and aging ovens. Come in the third day, and unload the thirty-six bars and pack the material for customer shipping. I have never had to even think about doing this, but it makes a good story, and when I tell it, shivers run up my wife's back.

I had promised Sandra two daughters. Well, after eighteen months of marriage little Nicholas arrived. Sixteen months later, I came through on half of my promise at least, when Alexandra was born. When Nick was in third grade, President Richard Nixon was having a great deal of trouble with his political career. During that period, Sandra and I went to a Parent/Teacher meeting at his school, and before the evening program they flashed students' art work and stories on a large screen in the auditorium. To our surprise, up came a story by Nick, which said:

When I grow up I am going to college. When I finish college,
I am going to go home, impeach father, and become president
of the aluminum company.

Nick has since graduated from Emory University, received his
M.B.A. from the University of North Carolina at Chapel Hill, and
worked the three years that I have required before any of the children
can join the business. Just to prove his prediction, Nick is now president of the extrusion company. He did not have to impeach his father.
He took the more direct route and fired him.

Travel

I AM NOT SURE WHEN MCDONALD'S STARTED FRANCHISING THEIR HAM-
burger places across the country, but I started selling the tools to manufacture aluminum storm windows in 1947. I also franchised dealers,
and had approximately one hundred and twenty-five in the U.S., thirty
across Canada, twelve in Europe, and one in Africa.

With this many outlets, a person is bound to run into some unusual
people, some unusual activities, and some just plain interesting facts of
life.

The man who bought my dealer program in Dublin, Ireland, was Ray
Ball. Ray lived with his wife, Laura, and two children in a very beautiful home outside the city. On our many trips to Europe, we always
made it a point to visit the Balls.

One year they invited us to be the guests of Laura's parents — the former lord mayor of Dublin and his wife — for dinner at their home. When we entered the lord mayor's home, we were surprised at the size of the rooms and at the number of people already in attendance. They were mostly "landed gentry" and their conversation led to race horses, for which Ireland is famous.

Although I had had some experience with horses, I never had any experience with the kind of racers that were being discussed, and Sandra and I stood out as "different." The lord mayor came over and started talking to us, and the next thing we knew we were up in his private study on the second floor, where he showed us pictures of some of his experiences as mayor.

There was a book of pictures taken in 1933 when our lord mayor was a guest at an American political function when an assassin attempted to kill President Roosevelt. The lord mayor of Dublin was on the stage with President Roosevelt and some other American dignitaries. The mayor of Chicago — Mayor Cermak — was shot and killed, but the president was not harmed.

Next, the lord mayor took us on a tour of his mansion. We went down a long hall on the first floor, which was made of stone walls and ceilings, and opened into rooms for laundry, ironing, baking, and cooking. There was a big, old, iron stove which looked like it could handle enough food for a hundred. Sandra and I found this all very interesting, and it certainly gave us an insight into how the higher echelon of Irish people lived.

Then, we heard the dinner bell and went upstairs to the dining room. To our surprise, the table seated seventy. The table itself was unusual as it was about four foot wide at each end, and expanded to twelve foot wide in the center so that the guests sat at an angle that made conversation easy. We had never experienced anything like it before, nor have we since. It was a wonderful dinner, and gave us a little insight into how to handle a table with seventy guests!

One of the jobs that Ray landed was replacing windows in all of the railroad hotels across Ireland. Most of these hotels were four stories high and had about fifty rooms. Ray took me around to quite a few, and I was always amazed that our Noecker windows were gracing the railroad hotels of Ireland.

Another dealer that we enjoyed visiting was Maurice Bewick in Newcastle, England. He was an importer of lumber from all over the world, and had a very large home.

On the side of his house was a room that was probably fifty feet long and twelve high, which was used for pool tables, card games, drinking, and smoking. In the lower corner of this room, a two hundred year-old, eight-inch thick grapevine grew fifty foot across the room, bearing large bunches of blue grapes in season.

The other interesting feature of his home was an open stairway from the living room to the second floor. Each stair was a four-inch thick slab of lumber made of different types of wood that started in a light color on the first stair and advanced to ebony at the top. I stood and gazed at these steps and asked my host if I could take a picture. I don't know where the picture is today.

From England I liked to cross the channel to Holland. Our Dutch dealer lived in a four hundred year-old home filled with bows and arrows, cannons, and other items used over the centuries for hunting. The walls were covered with wallpaper woven from cloth.

In the backyard was the largest aviary, or bird sanctuary, that I had ever seen. There must have been at least a thousand birds from around the world. This aviary project would have been considered a museum or a zoo if it was in our country. But here it was just a backyard interest.

When I asked the question, "How do you maintain a family home for four hundred years?" I was told that the Vandenbrink family followed the European practice of handing the home down to the oldest son in each generation. Then that son takes care of distributing the income from the property to his siblings. As we have heard, the second son is to go into the ministry, and the third into the army. I forgot where the fourth son and thereafter ended up.

The Vanenbrink family told me that they had been fortunate to have a son in each generation to handle the property, and since the present son is quite elderly, the family home is protected for at least two more generations as they felt their grandson was a fairly sexy young man.

The European dealer that we most enjoyed visiting was the late Andrew Whiteford in Edinburgh, Scotland. The family lived in a beautiful, large home on the shores of the *Firth of Forth*. I remembered as a kid that the Firth of Forth was one of my great repetitions. To think that I was sleeping in a second floor bedroom overlooking the Firth of Forth and beyond. I was told that on a clear day you could see oil stations out in the North Sea.

Even though I had never considered the Scots as great cooks, we visited a different restaurant on each trip. And of course, the stone fences that fill the countryside made me wonder if the population over the last thousand years had spent a good portion of their working lives stacking stones.

Andrew Whiteford had bought my window tool program thirty years before, and added our door and commercial window programs, working side by side with his wife, Mary. When Andrew died suddenly, Mary was able to take over. The Whitefords raised two wonderful sons, Colin and Neal.

In the winter of 1996 I planned my thirty-fourth trip to Europe to celebrate the retirement of the Edinburgh plant manager, Hugh Kenney. He and his wife, Millie, had become great friends to Sandra and me.

Our retirement party was held at the Prestonfield House, a magnificent gourmet restaurant with peacocks strutting around the yard. Drinks, appetizers, and your main course were served in small rooms to accommodate your own party. The entire restaurant was filled with antique furniture, and guests were encouraged to go from room to room to ogle. Truly royale!

Another very, very interesting dealer lived outside of London. We confidentially called him "our rich, rich dealer." He purchased a set of window and door tools and sold many storms windows and doors to the larger homes in "Castle Country." He had a title, and his wife also came from a titled family. On two different occasions he invited Sandra and me to his home.

The first was for dinner, which was served to us by a butler in tuxedo and white gloves. The home was filled with antiques, and attached to the bottoms of chests and dressers were pans which were filled with water to hydrate the air and keep the wood from splitting. In some of the rooms we felt as if the family ghosts were all around, watching everything we did.

The second time, we were invited for a weekend. On this visit we got into the kitchen, which was so large that it held a twenty-foot high children's swing set, as well as a large, iron stove, a refrigerator, dishwasher, and other appliances.

Many of their titled European friends were brought in to meet their American friends. We often laughed to think that they probably referred to us as the "rich, rich Americans" with no titles.

Sandra and I attended many world-wide trips with the Chief Executives Organization after that first visit to Canada soon after our marriage.

Our next trip with this group was to Puerto Rico. To make this trip a little more personal, we spent four or five days in Montego Bay, Jamaica, on our way to San Juan. Sandra is very fair skinned and after one day in the sun and wind, the skin on the back of her legs peeled and was very painful. But, we lived through it, and I remember that our dealer in San Juan, Mr. Nevarz, and his wife came over and spent an evening with us. This couple was from Spanish nobility, with both of their families coming to Puerto Rico about one hundred years before. This was about the same time that my ancestors traveled from Germany to the United States. We had a wonderful visit.

A few years later, the CEO group held a convention at the Costa del Sol in southern Spain. Sandra and I took Ann and Nancy with us on this trip, and we decided to give them the time of their lives.

I had made arrangements to fly from Marbella, in Spain, to Casablanca, in North Africa. We were then to take a bus to Marrakech. When we landed at Casablanca I was amazed at the condition of the airport. One of the airport doors was completely off, the other hung by hinges. I was told that American forces had built the airport during World War II, and that the country had money to maintain the runways, but not the building.

As we traveled by bus down desert roads, the sand swirled and local people moved by on little donkeys. We did see a few camels, but not many. In Marrakech, we found our little hotel and learned that its elevator carried only three people. We had a hard time deciding which one of us would stay on the ground floor with the luggage! Somehow, we managed.

We went out for a very nice dinner. I wore a pair of loafers with quarters stuck where pennies usually go. It seemed like twenty shoeshine men tried to shine my shoes on the way to the restaurant, commenting that I must be really rich to have silver coins in my shoes.

After we returned to the hotel, Nancy had a reaction to the shellfish we'd just eaten. She was having trouble breathing, and we knew she needed a doctor. It seemed that the hotel office closed at 10:00 P.M., but we were able to use the telephone. The telephone book, to my surprise, was one half in native tongue and the other half in English. I called several doctors who hung up when I could not communicate. Finally, I reached a woman who spoke a little English, and translated for her husband, a doctor. Within fifteen minutes he was at our door. We could not exchange a greeting with him, but the language of medicine must be universal as he understood Nancy's problem, took some pills out of his black bag, and within a few hours Nancy was feeling better.

We had decided to visit a mountain called "Ronda" on Costa del Sol, because this is where Christopher Columbus met Ferdinand and Isabella with his request to go to America. So, we rented a car, even though we had been told that in most places the road was only one lane wide. We were also told that the car descending had the right of way, with the car coming up having to back down to a wider space in the road for the first car to pass. As we wound our way uphill, we noticed perhaps a hundred cars that had hurled down the mountainside. Most, we were told, were left where they landed as there was no way to retrieve them. We did not find out what happened to the passengers. You can be sure that I drove with the utmost care as I did not want to spend eternity on a Spanish mountainside.

We were hungry when we reached the top, and as there were no restaurants, decided to have lunch at the home of a family who was willing to provide food. We went into a little courtyard and waited while they took the week's washing down off the line. We asked for Coke, and to our surprise, they had never heard of this drink.

A second mountaintop had been leveled off years before to be used as a prison for Spanish criminals. A drawbridge could be let down to deliver supplies or new prisoners.

We made it down the mountain without a problem, and have enjoyed memories of the site where Columbus was given his sailing orders by Ferdinand and Isabella.

Sandra and I made another day trip up a mountain near Marbella. We entered a church which we were told was the only one of its type in the world, serving both Muslim and Christian communities. We understand that in most cases Muslims face east in their worship, and Christians face west. To accommodate both groups, the seats are not pews, but flat benches for seating in either direction. The Muslims had their pulpit and altar at the east end of the church, the Christians had their altar on the west. In place of hymnals, they had twelve rather large boards, about twelve foot square, which were on the front near the pulpit. These boards were on hinges with the words for the songs and the music written on the board, so that when they were singing a certain hymn that board faced the worshippers. On one side of each board were the Christian music and words and on the other side of the same board were the words and music for the Muslim songs.

I know what I saw, but can't vouch for the histories and tales I was told.

St. Andrew's golf course in Scotland was our next destination, a wonderful CEO convention filled with history. Ann and Greg accompanied us on this trip, and friends Eppy Ledderer (Ann Landers), and her husband, Jules, were also there. A few years previous I was one of the sponsors for Jules Ledderer for admittance to the Young Presidents Organization. Therefore, we had a fine relationship on the trip.

We wondered how the Scottish dancers could have such spring in their ankles and knees until we learned that the dance floor was actually built on springs to help them with their jigs and high stepping.

At the end of our Scotland trip we went to Ireland to visit the Blarney Stone. This was an experience. We had to manuever on our backs to kiss the stone, with a fearful drop off a hundred-foot ledge if you were to slip.

I had window and door manufacturing dealers in Edinburgh, Belfast, and Dublin, so we tied in some wonderful business enjoyment.

The next interesting convention was held a few years later at London's Dorchester Hotel. We even had dinner with British Royalty, including sliding down the chute from the third to the first floor, which was a hair-raising experience for me.

A few years later in Switzerland, we had to take a cable car to mountaintop hotels near Bergenstock. Since I am afraid of heights, I will always remember the ride up the slope on what seemed like a seventy-five degree angle. And we had to make the trip three or four times a day.

Driving around the Swiss countryside we noticed exceptionally high corn and asked about it. We were told that during World War II American soldiers taking rest and relaxation in Switzerland noted the corn was very short, spindly, and the cobs were mediocre. A group of soldiers from Iowa told the Swiss farmers about Iowa-bred corn, and after the war, sent bushels of hybrid seed. Henry Wallace, President Roosevelt's Secretary of Agriculture, might even have been involved in the corn seed that found its way to Swiss soil.

Again, I know what I saw, but can't vouch for the histories and tales I was told.

A later convention was held in Munich, where Sandra and I took a bus trip down the north side of the Alps to Salzburg where the movie *The Sound of Music* was made. It is a city steeped in history. We were told that during World War II the American general and the German general reached an agreement that the Americans would not shell the city, and consequently, the Germans would do nothing to fortify, defend, or deface it. Salzburg was practically the only major European city that did not show major signs of wartime damage. The Swiss people set aside an area to honor the generals and their wives. Accordingly, four graves were established with monuments, and at the time we were there the American general, and the German wife, were in their tombs.

In 1988, my lovely wife, Sandra, noted that Northwest Airline was selling a trip to Hong Kong at very reasonable rates. We decided that we would take Nicholas and Alexandra, leaving the day after Christmas. This day was probably chosen as I had made my first trip to Europe on the same date in 1959.

As we approached the runway in Hong Kong, it looked as if we were making a landing on water. However, the wheels touched down, we landed, and explored the amazing city from end to end.

We took a side trip to Southern China, entering by way of Macao, which is where Marco Polo had landed hundreds of years before. Our trip over and back was made on a small boat which was supposedly propelled by a jet of air which hit the water at an angle. In Macao we were amazed by the height and by the prominent noses on several of the local people. We were told that seventeen of Marco Polo's men jumped ship, stayed in Macao, and married. Hence, the tallness and prominent features had remained through generations.

There were quite a few Chinese soldiers around the wharf at Macao, and I ended up buying a Chinese army cap for two dollars, which Sandra was sure I would be thrown in jail over. The hat and I both made it out of the country safely.

Michigan's Governor James Blanchard had appointed Michigan State professor, Dr. Wong, to sell the state's beans and cherries in Hong Kong, as he could speak both languages. I called Dr. Wong, and he and his wife took us to dinner at one of the nicer restaurants, and told us of his success in selling Michigan produce for Oriental dishes. He told us that the Traverse City cherries were amazingly successful because the Orientals appreciated the sour taste in the same way that other people of the world love peppery food.

The eating arrangement in China consisted of tables, all with eight chairs around them, and a "lazy susan" in the center with bowls of food from which everyone served themselves. Chopsticks replaced silverware. At home we had all four tried eating with chopsticks, and our method had been to level the plate on the table, and try to move the food from table to mouth, about eighteen inches. By the time we got our food to our mouths, it had always dropped off the chopsticks. We soon found out the people of China handle their plates and chopsticks differently. After putting food on their plates, they picked up the plates and held them within two or three inches of their mouths. The chopsticks were much more effective in that position. Again, we learned something from the Chinese.

Hong Kong and China provided us with life-long memories. On one trip, our driver took us out to a high, steep mountainside where a road was being built. Now, in our country we would have seen a dozen earth-moving machines scooping out loads of dirt, with each machine operated by one man. Here, there were six rows of people covering approximately one mile along the horizon. Every one had a shovel. The top row of six threw their dirt down to the fifth row, the fifth row to the fourth, and so on. Our driver thought there could be as many as three thousand people building this road around the mountain. Not one piece of machinery did we see. This gave us, particularly the children, another chance to appreciate America.

For me, the highlight of those great CEO trips was our ten days in Beijing, China in October of 1989. Our group of about fifty couples were really guests of Li Peng, the premier of China. Sandra and I were appointed an interpreter who stayed with us for our entire visit, a beautiful Chinese girl of about twenty-five, who spoke near-perfect English.We had trouble pronouncing her very Chinese name, so she said, "For this trip, I will adopt an American name. What are some American names that you like?" Sandra came up with some names, and our guide chose "Helen." We have kept in regular communication with her since the trip, and she is still Helen. She told us that she had finished three years of college and had been "hired" or "engaged" by the government.

Our guide, Helen, accompanied us on a trip to the Great Wall of China, to an area much further in than the average tourist was treated to. As I stood and gazed at this great structure, I realized that it had been built two hundred years before the birth of Christ. It extended through the countryside for about fifteen hundred miles, its many areas still in the same condition as it was when built some twenty-two hundred years ago.

On another day we were taken to XIAN. We got up at 4:00 A.M. to catch a 5:00 A.M. bus to an airfield where we were to leave for the seven-hundred-mile trip in a Chinese military plane. We were told that the airport did not have running lights, and so we had to wait an hour or more for daylight to take off. The trip was uneventful as airplane trips can be, except we commented on how the interior of the Russian aerofloat looked like our American airplanes and were told that yes, that was understandable because we had copied the Russian planes.

I think that almost everyone has read of the soldiers and horses that are terracato, each on an individual basis. The horses were as varied as Indian ponies to Clydesdales in our country, and the soldiers varied in appearance, size, and clothing as any you would see walking down a street in an American city.

It was surprising to me that these mounds had not been investigated earlier. There are four which appeared to be at least fifty to sixty feet high at the crest. A farmer had dug into one within the last century, discovering the horses and soldiers. The government had removed the dirt in this mound, and if my memory is correct, had removed the dirt around the horses and glued broken limbs back into their original positions. Our guides told us that the government had decided to leave the other three mounds to be opened at one-hundred-year intervals. This seemed kind of strange, but there have always been happenings, events, and conditions of the people of the world that have not been understandable to me.

As we spent the day wandering along the paths, viewing these terracato soldiers and horses, I would have expected many more tourists. Toward dusk we took the bus back to our plane. I became fearful of how we could land in the dark, as we had a three-hour flight and were leaving at dusk. But we landed without event. I could not understand the difference between no lights in the morning and lights after dark.

We were told not to expect to be able to take antiques out of China. Sandy had been a needle person for many years, and had done her homework before this trip. On the third floor of the state-controlled store in Beijing, she hit the jackpot when she found cases of antique embroidery. It took a very long time, but we found twenty-two to purchase at a cost of $640. They were on a yellow background, a color reserved for the royal family. Most had been worn on the sleeves of Chinese men and women. A few of the larger ones came from the backs of robes. We declared them at both the Chinese and American borders, and had no trouble getting them home. But the cost for framing was astronomical. I can't understand why Sandy can find bargains in China and not in Michigan.

Before we headed for home Helen told us that she would like to come to the U.S. to finish her education. Sandra and I had taken a liking to her, and told her we would do some investigating. Within a few weeks, my friend, Dave Hockenbrocht, had arranged a full scholarship, including board and room, at a small, western Michigan college. Helen was ecstatic and confirmed with her Chinese university how long it would take to earn her American degree.

I made arrangements for her transportation over, but the next word we heard from Helen was that her government would not grant her a visa to leave China. Even our American ambassador, Winston Lord, whom we had visited in Beijing could not secure the visa. We learned through the American consulate that the Chinese government did not give visas to their high-profile young people to come to the States, as it was a foregone conclusion that many of them would never return to China.

Memories: Family

ANYONE WHO HAS RAISED A GROUP OF CHILDREN HAS MEMORIES OF instances and situations that stand out — some important, and some just humorous.

In 1952 or 1953 I wanted to go to Washington, D.C. to check up on my patent applications, as at that time most of them were still in the form of claims. Chip and Ann were in grade school, so Harriet and I decided to take little Bill with us, and then go on to Florida for a two-week vacation. We left the older two with a maid of long-standing service and had no worry about their safety.

At that time, train was the method of transportation. The three of us traveled to Washington on the overnight train, and the next morning I visited the patent office while Harriet and little Bill played around the hotel. In the middle of the afternoon, we made our way by taxi to Grand

Central Station for our overnight trip to Miami. Harriet had purchased Bill a little beany hat with a windmill propeller on the top. At that time, Grand Central Station was loaded with pigeons, and little Bill, who was a very, very active four year old, ran after them with his windmill turning. I remember people by the dozens stopping to watch Bill as he chased the pigeons. It is funny how this little situation has always stayed in my mind as an interesting fact of raising kids.

We lost Harriet soon after Chip (Marshall Jr.) had started his college career at Dartmouth. A parents' weekend was the last real opportunity that he had to enjoy the company of his wonderful mother.

Upon the completion of his second year at Dartmouth, I suggested that I would finance a month of summer vacation in Europe. Chip found a young friend from Grosse Pointe High to go with him, and the two set off. Their "bible" was a little book called *Europe on $5 a Day.* Chip was determined to live on that sparse amount.

At the end of the summer, his friend returned to Michigan, and by prearrangement I was to meet my son in Nice, France, on the Riviera. After I arrived, it was his goal to continue living on *$5 a Day*, and I was to join that program.

We did find a small hotel in Monaco, the kingdom of Prince Ranier. We each had a small cot in a prison-sized room with a bath and shower down the hall. My recollection is that the cost of sleeping, bathing, shaving, and washing one's face and hands was one dollar per day for each of us. That left us four dollars for food, and we found a very adequate cafeteria on the Riviera where we took all of our meals. To Chip's satisfaction we each lived on thirty-five dollars for the week — which he felt was a tremendous accomplishment, and which I felt was meager living.

At the end of the week I went off to the United Kingdom to call on some of our dealers, while Chip stayed on the Riviera for another week.

I had made arrangements to meet him in London as he was going to be in England at the end of his trip. This was our second stay together in London, as he had accompanied me on my first trip there on the day after Christmas in 1959 when we established our first European dealer.

I checked into the Claridge Hotel and was waiting for Chip to arrive when I received a phone call from the doorman. He said that they had a young man who claimed to be my son and they wanted me to verify this. When I did, there was a long pause before the doorman said, "He is not dressed to enter our hotel. We will bring him up the service elevator at the back of the hotel."

When he arrived, Chip had a knapsack which looked like the type a bum would carry, a dirty face, unkept hair, and looked like quite a character. His shoes were the most worn-out pair I had ever seen. The heels were gone off both, the soles had large holes, and the stitching holding these soles to the toes had been torn out so that the soles were flapping in the air. We cleaned him up as best we could, fitted him into some of my clothes, and decided to go down for lunch. Again, at the dining room, they stopped us, and with some embarrassment told us that he was not dressed appropriately to dine there. After some discussion it was decided that they would admit him with a necktie and coat. My necktie worked out fine, but you can imagine what he looked like in my coat, as he was ten sizes smaller than me.

After our lunch at Claridge's, we went to Harrod's to buy him some new shoes. By British standards, his feet were too wide and too large. During the time we were trying to find a new pair, he asked the clerk if Harrod's could repair his old pair. The clerk brought over the department head and several other people — in jest, I think — and showed them Chip's shoes. As you can imagine, there seemed to be a great deal of humor generated among these Britishers. But, in typical British fashion, we were told in very nice terms that Harrod's considered these shoes beyond repair.

After some time we found a pair of shoes that fit. Later in the evening, Chip decided to throw his old shoes away, and into the wastebasket they went. Later, unbeknownst to him, I slipped them out of the wastebasket and hid them in my suitcase. The shoes returned to Michigan and were shown to quite a few of my friends — but not to his — as a humorous episode of his European summer.

Some months later, I hit upon the idea of having these worn-out shoes bronzed, as we already had his first pair of lace-up baby shoes bronzed and on display in our family home exhibit. I took the shoes down to the J.L. Hudson department store and into the bronze shoe department where I was told that they only bronzed baby shoes, and had never bronzed a size twelve D. I persisted as I felt that this was going to be a great Christmas present. The lady clerk brought out the department manager and several other employees from the same area, and ridiculed the shoes as unfit for bronzing. However, I persisted and they told me that they would bronze only one. Accordingly, I picked the worst one, if that was possible.One of the last steps that Chip had taken in this shoe was into a wad of British chewing gum which was flattened to about the size of a quarter, but definitely recognizable as a cud of gum. I asked them to include the gum in the bronzing.

One of Chip's most interesting Christmas gifts that year was the bronzed shoe, gum and all, with the following label:

MARSHALL NOECKER
12,500 MILES
EUROPE — SUMMER 1962

The bronzed shoe is in a permanent shelf display at our home, and almost every time we have a party, someone picks it up and it becomes a great topic of conversation.

During Chip's freshman year the college had a "date" weekend, and he invited his sister, Ann, to be his guest. At sixteen, she was the most beautiful girl to attend the weekend. I helped her select the "right" clothes.

The event took place in the middle of winter, and there is always a lot of snow and ice in Hanover. This was a "high heel" party for Ann, her first, and therefore, she wasn't accustomed to walking in the heels. As she entered the hallway, she slipped on her snow-covered heels. Her feet flew up in the air, and her body prone on the floor. What an embarrassment for a sixteen year old on her first "date." As with many situations, there was a silver lining. Chip says that for years, his friends at Dartmouth reminded him of his beautiful sister's "fall" into the party world.

In the meantime, through her political experience with me, Ann had learned that Mrs. George Romney held a very influential position with the American Field Service (AFS) student exchange program. Through this connection, and the fact that Ann was an outstanding student, she was chosen to study in Belgium in 1963.

Our good friends, Betty and Tom Fox, gave an evening cocktail and dinner party in honor of Ann's going away. At that particular time

"Velcro" was a new product, and Tom Fox made the most of this product by fastening the liquor bottles from his bar to a rather large tree in his backyard with strips of the stuff. After serving a guest, he would slap the bottle against the tree until it was needed for the next drink. Naturally, this was a great incentive for conversation.

When Ann arrived in Ninove, she was very pleased to be staying with Dr. and Mrs. Vander Hulst, who had three daughters and a son, all near her age. Dr. Vander Hulst was the personal physician to the royal family, and Ann had the pleasure of meeting Queen Wilhelmina and her children.

When Ann came home I remember asking her, "Did your French improve a lot?" Her reply was, "No. But their English sure did!"

When I first came to Michigan in the late 1940s, I realized that I needed to fit into the business and professional life of the community, and enrolled in the Dale Carnegie class. I soon learned that in making a speech, the first few words uttered sets the tone for the presentation. The goal is to get the audience with you. I also learned that it is very common for a speaker to have decoys in the audience to help with this.

When Ann graduated from the Grosse Pointe High School, I was privileged to be asked to deliver the commencement address. To me, this was the biggest responsibility that I had ever had, as I knew this presentation had to be outstanding so that I would not embarrass my darling Ann. I fell back on Dale Carnegie and placed three decoys in the audience. A great friend and right hand man, Dave Padilla, took the rear of the auditorium. Two other coworkers took a side. Together we devised a system. One, when they raised their right hands everything was going fine. Two, when they raised their left hands, I had to speak louder. Three, when they shook their left hands, I was too loud. Four, when they shook their right hands, I was talking too fast. This system must have worked out as there were approximately eight hundred in the graduating class, and Ann was the heroine of the day.

Ann, my lovely little girl who had accompanied me on my political endeavors, was soon ready to make her application for college. She chose eight schools, and instead of listening to me and not mentioning to each of these schools that she had made other applications, she felt she had to be honest and no matter what I said, she was going to tell each of these eight that she had applied to seven others and named the seven.

In the process of looking at colleges Ann and a girlfriend, who is now a doctor, Dr. Carol Quinn, wanted to check out Purdue University as they both had applied there. At that time, Ann was just learning to drive and the plan was for her to do all the driving from Grosse Pointe to Purdue and back. We got into Indiana where there is a large Mennonite settlement and many horses and buggies on the road. Ann was driving too fast, sixty and sixty-five miles per hour. I tried to talk her into slowing down, and her comment was, "The sign says sixty-five miles per hour and that is what I'm doing." Well, it took a little arguing, but she slowed down and we saved all those horses.

The college administrator told us that there was a party for prospective students that evening at the union building. We went to our rooms, and the girls spent hours getting dressed and made up to attend this affair. When they came back afterwards we laughed for a long time about what they thought of the boys who had been accepted at Purdue. The boys did not sell these two on the college.

Ann was accepted at seven colleges, and chose the University of Michigan, because before her mother died she asked Ann to look after me. Ann felt that being in Ann Arbor, she was close enough to get home every weekend.

One thing that we did before Ann left for the University was that I tried to help her prepare her wardrobe. I had no relative within 1,250 miles who was able and willing to help us, and accordingly, I was the chooser of the wardrobe. I made every mistake that a parent can, choosing suits that possibly a forty year-old lady would wear, coats that were full length, and shoes that looked like old ladies' clompers. So, while she went off to school with beautiful clothes, none were acceptable for a freshman girl. I learned my lesson in shopping for clothes for my college-age children.

The University of Michigan had an exchange program with the University of Sheffield in England for the second half of students' junior year. Ann wanted to go. I felt protective, but finally said, "yes." Her plan was to travel with a girlfriend on a little ship called "The Seven Seas," which at that time was used to transport high school and college students around the world. I remember flying with Ann to New

York City. We stayed in a hotel, and the next morning I took her to the dock to see "The Seven Seas." It was small, and not in the best condition, and I had a very difficult time deciding whether I should let my little Ann spend the next seven days crossing the Atlantic. I talked to my God with Ann, and the three of us decided that "nothing ventured, nothing gained." She would make the trip. On my way back to Detroit, I was probably the most nervous person on the plane as I was sure I had made a mistake in letting her go. Seven days later, I heard from Ann in London.

At Thanksgiving, 1965, I introduced little Nancy, who was just ten, and Ann to Sandra at a dinner for the three of us with Sandra's parents on Grosse Isle. Their mother had been sick for five years, since Nancy's birth, and another five years had passed since her death. I am sure that if this lapsed time had been much shorter that my children would have had some objection to me remarrying. But, they all decided that it was the best thing for me, and they all loved Sandra as a prospective mother. So this dinner was a highlight.

At the end of four years, when Ann's diploma came through from the University of Michigan, we were surprised as it said her graduation "was with highest honors." She had been a near-perfect student.

By 1967 we had another child deciding on college. Bill had heard that Cornell University in Ithaca, New York, was comparable in hockey to the position that the University of Michigan enjoyed in football. Therefore, his number one choice was Cornell.

I have always felt that a one-on-one method in every business transaction was the only way to go, so Sandra and I decided to take Bill to Cornell to make an application in person. We met with the admittance counselor, and since Bill's grades were outstanding in high school, he had no problem in meeting the academic requirements. But, his real interest was in the hockey program. We were sent to the athletic department and met the hockey coach. I remember specifically that when the coach asked Bill how much hockey he had played, Bill's comment was, "I think I have been in about four hundred hockey games. I started playing hockey in the third grade, and I have played on dozens of teams since."

The hockey coach's answer was, "I don't think I have ever interviewed a prospective player who has four hundred hockey games behind him. I look with favor upon you, and if Cornell University accepts you from an academic standpoint, we will work on the hockey program."

We all drove home with happiness on our faces. Bill enjoyed an exciting and interesting four years at Cornell, although he was continuously bothered by the prospect of being drafted for the Viet Nam War. In retrospect, Sandra has always said that if Bill's number came up, she would have taken him to Canada to escape that worthless war.

When Bill graduated, there was great talk and plans for another hockey league. Bill had two invitations to try out for this new league — one from the Michigan Stags, and the other from the Hartford (Connecticut) Whalers. This looked like a great opportunity for him to continue to enjoy hockey. However, it was my opinion that this hockey expansion league might not be successful, and possibly before the year was out he would be without a job and probably be owed salary for his work. Sandra and I spent hours suggesting that he forget the athletic experience and secure his M.B.A.. We finally won out, but in the many years since, I have often felt that in Bill's opinion he missed a wonderful opportunity.

Bill went to work on his M.B.A. at the University of Michigan, and after two years, accepted a job with one of the Big Eight C.P.A. firms, and soon thereafter became a Certified Public Accountant.

Six years later, little Nancy was ready for college. When Nancy lost her mother she was a mere babe, and I have all of the wonderful memories of her growing up. At that time, we lived in a rather large house with three bedrooms on the first floor and several on the second. Nancy was in the bedroom across the hall from me, and I can still hear her little feet padding on the floor as she ran to jump into bed with me in the middle of the night. I was her security blanket.

Now, she was ready for college. She had excellent grades and was accepted at Michigan State University in Lansing. I can still remember that Sandra and I took her to Lansing for registration and the first day of classes. Little Alex was a babe at that time, and she went with us to see her sister off. There was a big, loving arrangement between Nancy and her little sister.

Nancy enjoyed two years at Michigan State University with very excellent grades, but felt she was not in the program that she should be pursuing. When it came time to enroll for a third year, she hesitated, then took a job as a housesitter in Ann Arbor, enrolling at the University of Michigan for a semester.

Her real interest was in design work in the fashion world. There were two places to pursue this — New York City or Los Angeles. She chose the latter and continued her education at a Design School in California. She was also a part-time student at U.C.L.A.

When Richard was ten years old he developed a real interest in Boy Scouts, and of course, since I was his new father and wanted to be successful in this field, I became an active Boy Scout supporter. We attended weekend events all over our area. In addition, there are all sorts of processes that a young scout must accomplish in order to become an Eagle Scout. Within a few years, Sandra and I proudly stood with our son, Rick, as he was awarded the badge of Eagle Scout.

Then Greg became very interested in scouting, and I went through the same process and the same responsibility with him. To our surprise, in a few years we again stood proudly with Greg as he was awarded the badge of Eagle Scout.

We learned that very, very few Eagle Scouts ever get into trouble with the law, with their church, or with their friends. We certainly have enjoyed this privilege with our two Eagle Scouts.

Richard did not have the interest in college that our other seven children enjoyed. His interest was in being a musician in his own right, and leading the group.

His entrepreneurial experience went back to the sixth grade. One day Sandra received a call from the principal of the junior high school. He wanted Sandra and me to come to his office at nine the next morning, but didn't tell her exactly what the problem was. He did tell her that it involved Rick.

When we arrived the next morning, we learned that Rick had found an old *Playboy* magazine, had cut out all the interesting pages, and was selling them to other sixth graders — both boys and girls — for fifty cents a sheet. We assured the principal that the sales would stop.

When we got home, Sandra called her mother, who was livid. Sandra's mother then called Sandra's father, a bank president, and told him that they were going up to Grosse Pointe to straighten out this grandson. When they arrived at our house at about three that afternoon, Sandra's mother still had not told her husband what Rick's problem was. The proposed solution was that Rick and his grandfather go to Rick's bedroom where he would tell his grandfather the story.

You can just imagine how the president of a bank would react to a grandson who was making money, albeit in an unusual way. He was proud of the boy, and could not keep a straight face while scolding him. For the next ten years Sandra, her parents, and I laughed every time a reference was made to Rick's talent as an entrepreneur.

Rick was an excellent student, and to our surprise and the surprise of his teachers and principals at the Grosse Pointe High School, he had enough credits to finish high school in three years. He was the type of young man that the high school thought should go on to college, but...no way. So, he led a band for a couple years until we decided he would starve as a musician. We would take him to England to work for me in one of our factories for six months — to enjoy the glories of being an entrepreneur in his own right.

A few weeks later we arrived in London where Sandra, Rick, and I spent four or five days visiting all of the outstanding museums and points of interest. Overnight, Rick learned where music was being played in London, and on our last evening we all went to a place called "Ronnie Scott's," where several bands from all over Europe came to play. The next evening we flew up to New Castle where I had a small factory, introduced Rick to the manager, and made arrangements for him to live at the home of one of the employees. We thought he was set for life.

Six months later, on Valentine's Day, his six months were up and I met him at the Detroit airport. When we got home, I opened a bottle of champagne and Sandra and I were enjoying our first glass with our young son whom we thought was now going to pursue a career as a factory manager. Halfway through the drink, Rick came over, put his arm around me and said, "Father, you couldn't have done more for me than you have in these last six months under any circumstances. I learned more about music in this period than I could have in a lifetime in the United States."

We asked him to explain, and he told us that every Friday night he had caught a plane in New Castle, arriving in London (about 270 miles) in time to play at Ronnie Scott's with a group, say, from Spain. On Saturday evening he'd play with a Czechoslovakian band, and on Sunday afternoon with a group from Poland. Monday mornings he would catch a 6:00 A.M. flight back to New Castle to spend the week working.

After twenty-four hours of discussion, the next evening Sandra and I told Rick that we would finance him for six months while he was reestablishing his music group.

The *Sun Messengers* was recognized as one of Michigan's best big bands, several times opening Detroit's Montreuz Jazz Festival. Rick was the leader, arranger, booker, and chief percussionist.

Later, Rick started another group called *Blues Insurgents*. This group of six musicians was invited to play opening day at the European Jazz Festival. Sandra and I were in Edinburgh, Scotland on business when we heard that Rick's group was on its way to Brussels. We canceled our trip home and flew to Brussels, arriving about an hour after the band members. They had rented a large van and were able to load their instruments and luggage, as well as Sandra and me, for the ride to our hotel.

Early the next morning, Sandra and I took one of the beautiful European trains one hundred and twenty-five miles, from Brussels to Breda, Holland. The *Blues Insurgents* opened at 2:00 P.M. to a crowd estimated at a hundred and twenty-five thousand. We enjoyed being with and near the group for three days. It was a great thrill, especially for Sandra, to have our son recognized as a world musician.

This group has since been invited back to play at the Festival, and has made several CDs under the *Black Magic* label at one of Europe's largest recording studios.

Although the money hasn't rolled in in a big fashion, the lifestyle has been adequate and very enjoyable for our musician.

Of all the children, Greg was sort of a leader in retaining what we might call "little-used information." For example, he knows more Biblical names, I am sure, than most ministers do. So, as Greg's graduation from high school approached, it became a problem of where to project his abilities.

Somewhere along the line, the United States Naval Academy at Annapolis became a possibility. Greg had many ancestors going back to our country's beginning who had served in the armies and navies during our wars. Sandra and I went with Greg to several meetings on Annapolis requirements, and it looked like he was going to be accepted. But, somewhere along the line, it came out that the day at Annapolis started at 5:00 A.M., and before we knew it, the Naval Academy was history.

Greg had several friends who were going to the University of Michigan in Ann Arbor, and he had no trouble being accepted into the Residential College, where the students live in the same area as the classes meet.

At the end of the first year, Greg and a friend came up with a great idea for making money. They heard that you could buy a pick-up truck, brand new in Detroit, drive it to Alaska, sell it to the workers in the Prudoe oil fields, and pick up approximately six to eight thousand dollars in profit. He figured that after three or four trips that summer, he would have approximately thirty thousand dollars to start his second year of college. It sounded too good to be true. But, I bought it.

I purchased a Plymouth Trailblazer for Greg, and his friend's father bought a Dodge Ram pick-up for his son. They drove to Alaska in six days, only to find that the Prudhoe project had been completed, and there were five thousand used pick-up trucks for sale. Greg and his friend ended up with two new trucks on their hands, and no cash in their pockets. Greg was too embarrassed to tell his family. So, to pick up some ready cash, he went to work on a Japanese fishing boat where his job was to cut the heads off of millions of herring. He did come home with ten fingers.

When it came time to return to Michigan, we found that Greg had made another discovery. This time it wasn't oil, it wasn't cash, and it wasn't fish. It was girls. Greg was twenty years old, and had met a young lady from Texas with a four-year-old son. She was twenty-four, but told Greg she was twenty-two. He told her that he was twenty-two. So, here we had a twenty-two year old, and a twenty-two year old, enjoying life in Alaska. You can probably understand why Greg was enjoying Alaska with little money. What twenty year-old young man would not think he had the best of two worlds? We even lost contact with him for several weeks.

We gave Greg an ultimatum — that he had to be home to continue his second year at the University of Michigan — only to find out that he had missed the deadline by weeks. Finally, he decided to start for home. Both his girlfriend and his friend who drove the other truck remained in Alaska. Greg got as far as Whitehorse in the Yukon Territory, where he rolled his nice, new Plymouth truck on a gravel road.

We received a call from a Canadian mounted policeman from Whitehorse, informing us that Greg was there with his damaged truck. Greg did not want to talk with us. The policeman also told us that several "homemade" mechanics were helping Greg make his truck drivable again — without a windshield. Greg got the truck moving, and the next day we heard from the mounted police that they followed Greg for the first fifty miles, and he seemed to be rolling along in good shape.

Next, he lost a wheel in Edmonton, Alberta, and we were able to arrange for him to stay with some acquaintances we knew through YPO. When a new wheel arrived, Greg was on his way again and made it as far as North Dakota where my family was still numerous. He spent some time with them, and we understood that some of my relatives gave him great assistance in making his vehicle drivable again. After three or four provisions of cash, the next we heard from Greg was from northern Indiana where he broke down again. Our daughter Ann's husband, Murray Dawson, went out from Chicago to see the truck and concluded that it should be scrapped and Greg should fly home. This he did.

As it was too late to register for his second year at the University of Michigan, and since we had lost the total value of a brand new Plymouth Trailblazer pick-up truck plus hundreds of dollars of financing Greg for the summer, it was determined that he would operate one of the extrusion presses for the remainder of the college year. We bought Greg an old pick-up truck which was parked in our driveway during the winter. Since Greg's shift started at 6:00 A.M., and he was more than an hour's drive away, between four and five o'clock every morning he roared the engine of this rather dilapidated pick-up truck. He wanted us to know that he was working out his "happy" summer. In due course, Greg received his degree from the University of Michigan.

Disney World has played a part in our life as a family with eight children.

When Chip went to work in New York City after graduating from Dartmouth, he invested in Disney stock, his first entry into the stock exchange. In a few years he sold his shares at a handsome profit.

Our family's next contact was a few years later when Sandra and I married. We tried our best to assimilate our two families successfully, and Disney World seemed to be a place to spend some time together. So, that first spring, we took Nancy, Greg, and Rick.

A few years later we took Alex and Nick with us to a Chief Executives Organization convention at Disney World because we thought that at two and three years, they were old enough to enjoy the trip. We had reservations at the hotel which the train stopped in, and had plans to jump on to visit the shows and exhibits.

Fate intervened. A few hours after our arrival we saw little pock marks on both Nick and Alexandra. We decided there was not much we could do, so we bought a full-sized rubber blanket, and each day we made a bed out on the sunny lawn at Disney World and spent the day with our babies, shading them from the sun so their chicken pox would not be exasperated. After two or three days, their pox seemed to clear up. So, on the last day we dressed them up in their cutest clothes and took them on a cruise aboard a flat boat which held our one hundred convention-goers. Nick and Alex were the stars of the convention, and you can imagine how proud Sandra and I were to provide the entertainment for the evening.

A few years later we decided to take Nick and Alex again, as they were the right age to enjoy all that Disney World had to offer. I remember one evening the four of us were going through the Ghost House. You ride in a cart which goes around a track, and all of a sudden a large ghost appears to be sitting in your cart with you. Nick jumped up and screamed, "I need my father for this." The next thing I knew I had Nick in my arms, hanging on around my neck, scared of the ghosts.

So these were our memories of Disney World.

Back in the early seventies, when Nick and Alex were ready for prekindergarten and kindergarten, there was much talk of bussing children around the school area to provide diversity in each school. In our particular case, my dear wife, Sandra, could not fathom the idea of her prize babies being transferred by bus for miles. Therefore, it was decided that we would make application to the University Liggett School, a private institution in our Grosse Pointe area. To our surprise, when we took them to Liggett to discuss entrance, we found that the lady in charge was a long-time family friend. So, in a few weeks, Nick and Alex started kindergarten and pre-kindergarten at Liggett.

By the time Nick was ready for the third grade, the bussing issue had dissipated and therefore, we decided to send him to our public school where the teacher proceeded to tell us that our son was so far ahead that she called him the "assistant teacher for the third grade." With that explanation, Nick returned to Liggett for the fourth grade and thereafter.

Liggett School held an annual Halloween party, and somewhere along the line I mentioned that Wayne State University had the largest mortuary science school in our area. So, Sandra and I were delegated the job of getting a coffin suitable to hold a body for the purpose of frightening the daylights out of the little kids.

I made arrangements with the Wayne State Mortuary Department for us to come in on a Saturday and choose a coffin from their rather large and elaborate collection, which was stored in a basement room. It seems that over the years Detroiters died in many places in the world. Consequently, there were coffins from India, Africa, Iceland, Antarctica, and other odd places. Sandra and I chose a coffin from India which we thought would be adequate for our Halloween exhibit, particularly so, since it was completely black on the inside as well as on the outside. We had borrowed a station wagon, and the sole employee who was working on Saturday agreed to help me carry the coffin to our wagon.

We drove down the expressway the fifteen miles from Wayne State to the Liggett School with about three foot of black coffin hanging out the back of our friend's station wagon. We are sure that many people followed us just to see what we were going to do with the "body."

Nicholas graduated from Liggett with a very high standing in his class and was a National Merit Scholar. Alexandra graduated the next year.

Four outstanding sculptures cast in bronze by Bernice Carmichael and presented to Sandra and Marshall. Left to right: Two little girls (Bernice's daughters); Secretariat, the racehorse that won the Triple Crown; a male penguin sitting on an egg; and our son Nicholas, at two years of age.

Above: Marshall and brother Raymond touring Detroit in Marshall's 1953 MG-TF1500.

Below: The Noecker brothers touring North Dakota on the family Harley Davidson.

Sandra and son Richard, who is an international musician with his group, Johnnie Bassett and the Blues Insurgents. Their field of entertainment is the entire United States, Canada, and Europe.

Marshall with two leaders of the world: Mr. Lutz (center) and Tony Speller (right).

With daughters Nancy, Ann, and Alexandra.

Four of our children: Marshall, Nancy, Ann, and William.

Everyone at home for the wedding of Alexandra and Dr. Richard Ferrara II.

Enjoying a family reunion on Siesta Key in 1991. Everyone is wearing a sweat shirt from the alma mater.

A family dinner in 1994. Home for the holidays.

The Noecker men: Marshall; Marshall Raymond; Richard; Nicholas; Gregory and son, Duncan; Murray Dawson (Ann's husband); Bill and son, Drew.

Marshall and Sandra at home in the family dining room.

Alexandra and Nicholas enjoying a weekend at the Grand Hotel on
Mackinaw Island, Michigan, with their parents.

Harriet playing with Chip and Ann on the sand dunes of western Michigan.

Nancy's high school graduation.

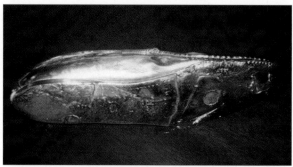

Shoe worn by Marshall (Chip) on 12,500-mile trek throughout Europe after his first year of college.

Marshall presenting his oldest grandchild, Dana Noecker, with a diamond ring from her Grandmother Harriet's wedding ring.

A family portrait.

Grandson Richard Ferrara III truckin' sand on Siesta Key, Florida.

Top: Granddaughter Lauren Dawson next to Noecker tombstone.

Left: Granddaughter Lauren Dawson next to Brock tombstone.

Merrilee and Greg's wedding. Alexandra and Nicholas on the ends.
St. James Lutheran Church.

Marshall relaxing in Florida home with Drew and Bill.

It's a Long, Hard Climb to the Top!

Top: Nicholas and Alexandra.

Bottom: Nicholas. He started swinging early.

To Succeed, You Must Keep Your Eye on the Ball!

Top: Marshall with granddaughters Leah Noecker and
Victoria Spangler.

Below: One of the factories.

VOLUME 6
NUMBER 2

MAY
1989

Michigan
Business

Collectively, Nick and Alex had twenty-six years of private education at Liggett, which cost me a fortune. So, when I add those twenty-six years to the thirty-five years of college, it equals sixty-one years of tuition that Sandra and I paid in raising our family.

Nick chose Emory University in Atlanta and spent four very profitable, interesting, and productive years. He enjoyed hockey and was instrumental in forming a college team at Emory, and then establishing a seven-college hockey league as a new sport in the South.

He continued his education with a Master's degree in business from the University of North Carolina at Chapel Hill. We understood from him that he was the youngest student in the M.B.A. class, which did not surprise us.

After considerable investigating, Alexandra decided on Babson College in Boston to pursue her interest in international business. In due course, and after several large and interesting parties, she received her degree.

On her twenty-first birthday, Sandra and I made arrangements to throw a birthday party for Alexandra at the Harvard Club in Boston. This was a gala affair, and our "princess" was the belle of the ball. Over one hundred and twenty friends attended her party, and we would have to say that the Harvard Club did her justice.

Babson College offered a program on entrepreneurial studies and awarded five thousand dollars to the junior who put together the most satisfying business program. To our surprise, but not amazement, Alex won the Phillip Charm Prize for her study of a small manufacturing facility that made parts for commercial fishing. I suggested that this sum be used on her last year at Babson, but I was quickly reminded that the other girls had not had any earnings to help support their college careers. Accordingly, her mother and I were soft hearted, and Alex spent that summer studying in Italy at the University of Rome.

Alex surprised us again by pursuing her Master in Business Administration. From college guides we had a list of the top twenty M.B.A. schools which included her brother Chip's Dartmouth, her brother Bill's University of Michigan, and her brother Nick's University of North Carolina. The second list of twenty M.B.A.

schools from our college guide started with Southern Methodist University (SMU) in Dallas. Alexandra thought it was better to be number one in the second group of twenty, and therefore, after two interesting and enlightening years in Dallas, she received her M.B.A. in International Business from SMU.

In 1980 Alex Haley set the world to thinking about *Roots*. I relished the book and then the movie. I have always had a great interest in my blood relatives. I guess this was sparked by the fact that my father, with nine brothers and sisters, and my mother, with six brothers and sisters, were all rather closely knit in our region of North Dakota.

As kids, we played with our cousins. We knew the problems that our uncles and aunts were having, and as I look back on it, they generally did not conceive of divorce. We didn't know what divorces were. However, when we came to my generation, I had some cousins who wanted to "try greener pastures."

My interest in family peaked when I formulated a questionnaire to determine a family tree of blood relatives with updates on what they were doing with their lives. I knew all of my cousins on my mother's side, the Brock family, as we had grown up within a twenty-mile radius, and surprisingly, all the brothers and sisters were friendly.

I sent the questionnaire to each of my cousins on my mother's side, twenty-two in all. I told them what I wanted, and to my surprise, everyone sent back their sheets providing me with the pertinent information on their children, and their children's children. In the olden days, family histories were kept in the family bibles. I received many faxed copies of bible entries. There were even one or two babies recorded in the sixth generation.

People have different needs for sleep, and Sandra and I were no exception with her needing eight hours while I was getting by on about six. Therefore, after she went to bed, I stretched my family data out on the breakfast bar and went to work. The information from one hundred and thirty-six blood relatives had to be correlated so that it appeared to be one person's dissertation.

My daughter, Ann, was so interested in this project that she went to Germany to dig up some of the family history. She came back with stories from bibles and other records dating back to 1750. So, we were able to trace my mother's relatives back nearly two hundred and fifty years.

I was fortunate to find several old history books with many illustrations depicting life in Europe. I was able to transfer pictures of horses pulling plows, German maidens stacking hay, German frauleins making sauerkraut, and others to identify each person's page. For those who had large families, I showed rabbits. On the pages of those who were divorced, I showed two roosters or two lions fighting. As I finished the book, Sandra assured me that I would have a lot of unhappy relatives who would not be pleased to have been identified with rabbits or with fighting roosters. But, to my surprise when I sent the book out, not one complaint did I hear. On the other hand, almost everyone sent me a humorous note on their presentation.

In 1980, just one hundred years after my grandparents came to the United States, I sent this book out to their one hundred and twenty-two blood relatives as a gift. The responses to this work of love made it all worthwhile.

I had such success with my research on the Brock family that I decided to do the same with the Noeckers. I had twenty-four cousins in my father's family, and since he was the youngest of ten children, and five years younger than his preceding brother, many of these cousins were literally a generation older than me. Consequently, the sixth generation had fifteen members. When I got ready to put the book together, my grandson Drew was born, on July 29, 1981. Since the book was ready to publish, I wrote his entry in by hand.

In the Noecker family, I had one cousin who did not participate. For his page, I found a picture of a great big man sleeping behind a haystack and captioned it "Carson Sleepeth." When I sent the book out, Carson was the first I heard from. He called to say, "Had I known that this book was going to be this wonderful, I would have been the first to help you."

My comment was, "Carson Sleepeth."

I started the work on the Brock book during the 1980 Christmas holidays and completed the Noecker book on July 29, 1981, on the day of my grandson's birth. I wrote two books in seven months.

As I grew up in North Dakota, I visited the Noecker cemetery on a regular basis while my parents cared for the family graves. After my grandparents, Leo and Amelia Noecker, buried their little Amelia on a hillside facing west, there were requests for other burials, and so they established the Fairview Cemetery. Since the area was divided equally between Catholics and Protestants, my grandfather deeded ten acres to the Catholics and ten acres to the Protestants, side by side.

Back at this time there was a great deal of hostility between the two religions, and intermarriage in Dakota territory was infrequent as both sides held their group to be superior in religious philosophy. A few years later, the Catholics built a high, wire fence between their cemetery and the Protestant area. This fence stayed for approximately sixty years, and then the Catholics removed it. Now the two cemeteries are still side by side, and the area can be traversed on foot from the Catholic side to the Protestant side.

The Noecker tombstone is a granite hunk with a sixteen-inch ball on the top. I have been taking my grandchildren to North Dakota for the Fourth of July when each one turns nine years of age, and taken their picture standing by the Noecker tombstone.

When I was writing my family-tree book on the Noecker family, Ann went to Germany to research our roots, and to our surprise, came back with photographs of family tombstones which were exactly the same as the North Dakota tombstone. This was Ann's second trip to Germany to investigate our family history. She made one trip for the Brocks, and one trip for the Noeckers.

Later, in 1985, Sandra and I were invited to a Noecker family reunion near Stratford, Ontario, which was attended by several hundred blood relatives. These Noeckers were descendants of the two daughters and three sons who made their home in Canada after their mother took them out of Germany, while others, including my grandfather, settled in North Dakota and Iowa.

Sandra and I slept at a motel on the eve proceeding the reunion, and in the morning called a relative to ask where our ancestors had been buried. To our complete surprise and amazement, when we entered this cemetery we saw a tombstone that looked exactly the same as the one that my grandfather, Leo Noecker, had placed in North Dakota. It was also identical to the family monument that Ann photographed in Germany. This proved to us that there is a great family heritage, even when it comes to tombstones.

Family celebrations are often the most important part of family relationships. Our family is no exception.

Over the 1989-1990 holidays, Sandra and I decided to have a family reunion in Florida. We rented several condos for two to three weeks which were shared by Chip's, Ann's, Bill's, Greg's, and Nancy's families. Rick, Nick, and Alex were our guests at our condo.

Family reunions are wonderful! We ate a lot of German food, danced to German music, and it seemed that all of our activities centered on German traditions.

We took some beautiful pictures. Sandra and I made a collage of our family enjoying the water and the beach. This collage covers a good part of the wall over our breakfast table in Florida.

Sandra had the idea of a family photograph with everyone wearing a sweatshirt from the college they attended. Almost all of the children had attended a different college or university, and their spouses did not double up either. With five advanced degrees in the group, we had about twenty different sweatshirts. This photo became our 1991 Christmas card.

Later that year, on December 28, 1990, Sandra and I celebrated our twenty-fifth anniversary. We again rented several condominiums for our family group, and twenty-one members were together for the Christmas holidays in Florida.

To top off this great family vacation, our eight children presented Sandra and me with an eight-day trip on the Horizon luxury liner through the Caribbean. We boarded in San Juan, Puerto Rico.

We had been out three days when the Desert Storm War began. There were only three television sets on the ship and seven hundred passengers. We could not get close to a TV until about 3:00 A.M. when the "old" people went to sleep. Then we stayed with it until 6:00 A.M.

At the end of our cruise, arriving back in San Juan, we learned that Eastern Airlines was on strike. There were twelve thousand people stranded in Puerto Rico who wanted to get back to the States, and only a few flights a day on another airline. I learned that there were unscheduled flights, but that it would be seven to ten days before everyone could get on one.

Sandra and I decided to stay at the airport and take our chances getting out on one of the unscheduled flights. Eighteen hours later we were on a 737 headed for somewhere in New Jersey. When we arrived at approximately 2:00 A.M., the airport was virtually closed. I found a telephone and called for a hotel room. Then I called a cab company and was told that they didn't serve the airport from midnight to 6:00 A.M. I convinced the operator to send a cab to pick us up two blocks down on a street corner. We carried our bags to the designated spot and a cab was waiting. As we drove away, the driver told us that he was from Iran. Immediately we realized that the Desert Storm war had begun only a few days before. We squeezed each others' hands in the back seat and were numb. About a mile into our trip he told us that he had to stop and get directions to our hotel. We could see the hotel's electric sign and told him so. He said that he still needed to get directions because we had to get across the river. He stopped at a rather sleazy bar, and for the fifteen minutes we were left in the cab, we were quite frightened. He emerged and drove us to the hotel. We never did see a river.

On our flight from San Juan most of the passengers were older ladies with a lot of baggage. We felt guilty to think that we were enjoying a good night's sleep at a hotel while those poor ladies were probably sitting in the darkened airport all night.

Another memorable family tradition was established on each of our four oldest granddaughters' fifteenth birthdays when the girls were presented with rings made from diamonds from my first wife, Harriet's, ring. At the time of her death I decided that Harriet should be buried with her wedding ring, which was a traditional piece with five small diamonds in a row. Her engagement-type ring, the large diamond given to us by Harriet's step-grandmother in Biloxi, Mississippi, had two smaller diamonds on each side. I kept the ring until five years after Harriet's death, at which time I gave Ann the large diamond and had the four smaller ones removed. I decided to give each of my four oldest granddaughters one of these diamonds mounted in a white gold ring. Our first granddaughter, Dana Noecker, was presented with her ring on her fifteenth birthday at a celebration in Boston. Over the years since, Lindsey Noecker, Lauren Dawson, and Tishia Dawson have received their "first" diamond rings on their fifteenth birthdays.

Eighteen

Memories: Friends

FRIENDSHIPS ARE A WONDERFUL EXPERIENCE, AND MORE SO WHEN THEY continue throughout a lifetime.

Grosse Point was a relatively small, residential community, and many of the residents knew one another by sight, if not as friends. In my single years, it was my custom to work five to six hours at the office on Saturday, and I used the late afternoon to do my grocery, meat, fish, and sundry shopping for the week. My favorite small store was Verbrugge's Market, and I soon became a fast friend of the owner.

Since fish cannot be kept over the weekend, I always had a choice of many varieties for Sunday dinner. Marie and Molly, who were helping in my household, knew how to cook fish. Often these fish meals were "courtesy" and always at "wholesale." But one day Mr. Verbrugge came up with a good idea. We could, in effect, eat dinner with the Henry Ford family as he had just cut four steaks for them. He would cut the next steaks for us. I said, "Go ahead." Mr. Verbrugge wanted to be in on the dinners, so to us, they were his contribution.

One Saturday I was in the grocery store when I recognized one of the leading ladies of the Farms picking up a quart box of strawberries. She asked the clerk for the price, to which she replied, "Too much!" and set the box down. I bought the box and that night at dinner the children and I enjoyed strawberries that Henry Ford could have eaten.

You can imagine the hilarity at some of our dinners. Preteens and teens enjoy this sort of fun.

During my single years, Ann Landers (or Eppy Ledderer as I knew her), was to give a speech to the Rotary Club in San Juan, Puerto Rico, and for some reason invited me to accompany her, which I willingly and joyfully did. I remember a story that she told to this group that is unusual and maybe even funny -

> "In a hotel lobby a man was sitting reading a newspaper. Another man came along and sat nearby taking out his newspaper and reading. The first man dropped his newspaper and said to the second man, 'excuse me, but can you tell me what a woman's yet is?' The second man thought, laid his paper down, thought for a little while longer, and asked, 'I am a doctor and I can't answer your question. Why do you ask?' The first man picked up his paper and said, 'It says here, her husband shot her, and the bullet is in her yet.'"

Another old friend, Aleg Cassini, descended from Russian nobility who came to the U.S. before World War II. I worked a short time with him on the Alpha and Omega parts for the atom bomb that ended World War II. He then became a ladies' fashion designer and clothed Jackie Kennedy during her years in the White House.

My family and I have been lucky to have very special friends who have influenced our lives, added to our possessions, or directed our lives in a special way. Two of the special friends who come to my mind are Curtis and Bernice Carmichael. Curtis and I go back to the mid-fifties in the Young Presidents Organization. Both Bernice and Curtis held my hand when Sandra and I were married.

One year after our marriage, baby Nicholas joined our family. When Nick was about two years old, Bernice Carmichael, a talented sculptress and portrait painter of international fame, came to us and said, "We did not give you a wedding present, and I would like to sculpt Nick's head as our gift."

Sandra and I imagined that a sculptress worked with a live model day after day, until the work was completed. Now, Nick was an active two year old. He never learned to walk — instead he ran everywhere. We shared our concern with Bernice.

We soon learned how artists work. Bernice said she would take sixteen pictures of Nick, starting with a straight face shot. Then she would move to the right about twenty-two degrees for another photo, and keep moving until she had circled him.

Then Bernice posted four consecutive photos on each of the four walls of her studio. She used several follow-up visits to touch-up Nick's curls (his head was full of them), and to get the depth required for his eyes, ears, and other features.

We were asked for our stamp of approval, and it was probably the quickest she received in her career.

As we soon learned, the clay head was sent to a foundry where six bronze heads were cast. Bernice's philosophy was to never have more than six of any of her work cast so that the value was maintained. We were given one for our home and one to save for Nick, and Bernice kept one. We understand the other three went to museums in Paris, New York, and Detroit.

About the same time in our history, Bernice was president of the Scarab Club, which is a social and work spot for local artists. She mentioned that the ladies room was a disgrace. The Carmichaels and the Noeckers decided that fixing it up would be a fun project. We started with wallpaper of nude women that Bernice had found in Paris. Only the French could depict nude women as illustrated on these rolls of paper. Bernice will be remembered not only for being an outstanding artists, but also as the first female member, and first female president of the Scarab Club. And she will always have the distinction of leaving the club with the world's most humorous ladies room.

A few weeks later, when the project was completed, the artists scheduled a costume party at which Sandra and I were to "unveil" the ladies room. As so often happens, we had another function the same evening — the wedding of our good friends Robert and Muriel Smith's daughter, Gayle. The wedding was a black-tie event. We made a plan to attend both. Artists are generally late starters, so we would stay at the wedding until about nine o'clock, then change into costume for the second affair. Unfortunately, the wedding party occupied the restrooms at the reception, so we decided to park our car in the furthest and darkest corner of the parking lot to change. All went according to plan, until we were stripped down to underpants, shorts, brassiere, and nothing else. Around the corner came a car, and as the lights caught us, the occupants thought "something" was going on. They backed up for a second look. We dressed in costume as best we could, and when the curious sightseers drove off, so did we. Sandra maintains that this was the worst idea I ever talked her into.

During one of my trips to Europe I was honored at a luncheon by members of the Barclay Bank, which was the financial support for our European operations. At this luncheon, I was privileged to meet a member of the British Parliament — the Honorable Anthony Speller. We soon became close and intimate friends and enjoyed a wonderful business and social relationship.

I asked Mr. Speller to come to Detroit in the early 1970s as a luncheon speaker to raise funds for the candidacy of my good friend, U.S. Congressman Robert Huber. We held this luncheon at the Dearborn Inn, and to everyone's surprise, had a full house and raised the largest sum at a single event during his campaign. It seemed that Michiganders were very interested in hearing the words of a member of British Parliament.

Basking in the success of this luncheon, I invited Mr. Speller to speak at our Michigan '49ers dinner meeting (a follow-up to exit from the Young Presidents Organization) at the Country Club of Detroit. Mr. Speller accepted, and brought his lovely wife, Maureen, along.

We soon learned that Mrs. Speller had the assignment from the British government to keep the Shakespearean theater alive and well in the British Empire. At our Country Club of Detroit meeting Maureen enlarged on her activities around the world promoting Shaekspeare as a hero. Her presentation was accepted with a standing ovation.

Tony Speller was born in India, where his father was Director of Transportation, and sent back to England for school when he was twelve. Tony joined the foreign service himself, and was sent to Nigeria, where he met Maureen who was also serving. After five children, they were still a happy couple.

I have always thought it was surprising what a person can get, secure, or be favored with when he asks for what he wants. Accordingly, when our youngest daughter, Alexandra, was seventeen years old, I raised the point that we would like to have her work for a summer as a page in the British Parliament. Her mother would not think of letting our dear little girl spend the summer in London without parental supervision. So, we found a typical British flat in the London area with an address of "One Moscow Place." This flat could sleep seven, but the fifth, sixth, and seventh ones to arrive did not enjoy the luxuries of a Claridge Hotel. This summer in London gave us a chance to have some of the older children visit. On one occasion Chip, his wife, Carlee, their daughters Dana and Lindsey, and my niece Jenny Noecker from North Dakota, all came at the same time, making eight. Spaces five, six, and seven were occupied by the children, and I don't remember where number eight slept. But, we did live together for a week. Lindsey celebrated her twelfth birthday before Chip, his family, and Jenny departed for two weeks in Paris.

Over the years, Mr. and Mrs. Speller have enjoyed a several-week vacation every summer at our home on Siesta Key in Florida. But the summer following our stay in London, Tony and Maureen Speller were visiting with us in Grosse Pointe at the time the Faulkland Islands War between Argentina and Great Britain was waged. Tony had some responsibilities with the foreign empire, and twice daily he had to communicate with Margaret Thatcher's government on the status of this war as seen through U.S. eyes. Ten in the morning in the United Kingdom was 4:00 A.M. our time, and therefore, our telephone rang in the middle of the night. Discussions of his conversations, some directly with Margaret Thatcher, were the highlights of our family breakfasts.

A few years later, Mr. and Mrs. Speller's youngest daughter, Sophie, was engaged to be married to a young American from Maryland. We were invited to the London wedding, and decided to take Nicholas (who was a freshman at Emory University), and Alexandra (who was a senior in high school). We learned a great deal about British weddings — at least this particular wedding.

Instead of adult bridesmaids, five nieces and a nephew, ranging from fourteen years old down to two years old, marched down the aisle. Sophie was beautifully dressed and stood out with no competition from attendants (which in our country can be a problem if they are prettier than the bride). Instead, Sophie had twenty-five groomsmen, all dressed in tails and top hats, who formed a half moon around the bride. The ceremony took place in The Chapel of St. Mary Undercroft at the Palace of Westminster. The reception, including an eight-course dinner, was held in the Winston Churchill Room of the House of Commons Parliament building.

At the end of the dinner, the entire assembly went to the beautiful palace yard of the Parliament buildings where pictures were taken. In typical British fashion, a red-coated toastmaster stood on a platform, pounded with his staff, and announced the picture taking. First, the bride. Second, the bride and groom. Third, the bride, groom, and their parents. His ninth announcement was, "Now we will take the photograph of all foreigners." The four of us stood with a small group.

This was not the end of the wedding. Our family was staying in the Cadogan Hotel on Sloane Square. It seems that in the evening, about fifty young people had come to continue the wedding celebration. Somehow, they all ended up in the bar and recreation room of the Cadogan with Nick, who thought it only fitting that he should be the host for the late-night festivities. This bill was the largest that Sandra and I have ever paid for any public celebration.

Over our years of friendship with Tony Speller we have enjoyed, as spectators, many sessions of British Parliament, and learned that the origins of some common phrases originated there.

For example, the saying, "it is in the bag" has particular meaning in British Parliament. When a loyal subject of the queen or king wishes to deliver a petition to the monarch, it is placed in a velvet pouch (like a huge, open briefcase), which is suspended, waist-high, behind the chair of the Speaker. To this day, I'm not sure where the bag goes, but I think it goes, via the Speaker, to Buckingham Palace after the contents are checked.

The phrase "toe the line" goes back to the days when almost every member of Parliament carried a sword for protection. A pair of lines was drawn on the floor of Parliament at a distance where a member on one side, by keeping his toe behind his line, could not reach past the other line to inflict damage with his sword on an opposing member. These lines are still on the floor today. The swords are gone, but the Speaker will still tell an errant member who advances across the floor of the commons that "the honorable gentleman must toe the line!"

Another item may not be attributed to Parliament, but at least to the British. It has always been the custom for the British to serve ale by the pint or quart. In the olden days, the pub landlord kept a slate on which he noted how many pints or quarts each customer ordered. By the end of the evening, he paid and the "slate was wiped clean." The saying "mind your p's and q's" came from the customers checking the landlord's arithmetic. Hence both sayings originated in British pubs.

Taking basic arithmetic to a higher level than "p's and q's," early during my tenure in New Orleans, a friend told me that Tulane University was looking for a teacher for their Advanced Accounting class. I called the head of the business school, put on one of my three tailor-made suits, and headed off for an interview. This man welcomed me with open arms as he felt that my qualifications, including my work editing *Advanced Accounting Volumes 1 and 2*, made me superbly qualified. I was soon hired to teach the class two nights a week for two-hour sessions, using "my" text book. At the time, this class was the highest level accounting class the university offered and therefore was advertised as a "C.P.A. review" class.

Three years later I was living in Detroit again and interested in stamping out my territory — both in business and education. The C.P.A. field was still in its infancy.

When I called the University of Detroit and told them I was interested in teaching, my call was returned by Father Henry Wirtenberger S.J., Dean of Commerce, Night, and Law. When I entered his office a few days later, his leading comment to me was, "We were praying for a teacher for our top accounting class and the good Lord answered by sending you to see me."

I ended up getting the job teaching two nights a week, two-hour classes, for four years.

In order to liven up my classes at Tulane and at the University of Detroit, I tried to have a bit of advice to give my students at the end of each class which included:

▲ To have lunch with some of the older men who could give advice and instruction, rather than with their contemporaries.

▲ That if they went into business for themselves they should pick an older, experienced entrepreneur in the field to partner with. The partner would soon retire and they could take over the business.

▲ Always keep a clean, shaven face, wear a dress shirt and necktie, wear a pressed suit and shined shoes.

▲ Use good table manners, and always respond to a compliment.

To my surprise, the class members welcomed my bits of advice, and the final minutes of class were humorous and happy. In fact, one night after class one of my young students, Frank S. Moran, came to me with a question relative to my advice. He wanted to know if I knew a C.P.A. who was near the time of retirement. I happened to remember a young lady with the last name of Plante whom I had met in New Orleans during the war years. Her father was a C.P.A. in Detroit. I called him up and set up a lunch date for him, Frank, and myself. I think the finale of the story tells itself. Frank went to work for Mr. Plante, and in a few years the older C.P.A. retired. The firm became known as Plante and Moran and under Frank's leadership has grown to be the twelfth-largest accounting firm in the country.

After six years of teaching in universities, I enjoy meeting someone who was at one time my student. I always like to get his life's story.

Having grown up in a Lutheran family and community, I have always been cognizant that the place to be on Sunday morning is sitting in a pew at a Lutheran Church.

After a few years in Michigan, Pastor George Kurz learned that I was a C.P.A. and hit me up after a service to take over the responsibility of treasurer of his fledgling St. James Church in Grosse Pointe. He prevailed upon my dear wife, Harriet, for me to accept the position. I had just finished four years of teaching the C.P.A. review course at the University of Detroit and I certainly hesitated to take on another responsibility. But, religious pressure prevailed, and I accepted the job for one year.

The next thing I knew, the church was planning a building program to add a Sunday school wing and pastor's office, and I was in the middle of raising the money. In the early fifties, one hundred thousand dollars built a lot of church. Our building program required two hundred thousand, of which we were able to borrow half from a local bank through a leading church member who was affiliated with the institution. This left us with one hundred thousand to raise. With other church members, I hit upon the idea of selling bonds in one-thousand-dollar units to our members. To our surprise, we sold one hundred and five of the bonds, and when they came due, nearly every bond turned into a donation!

I recall that as a kid in North Dakota my father was treasurer of our little Lutheran church, and of the Fairview Cemetery which my grandfather Noecker started. I don't know how my dad became treasurer of both, but I remember that he kept the money in cash in two identical cardboard boxes stored on a top closet shelf. One was marked "Fairview," the other "Church."

While he was treasurer, he had the idea of getting church members to take a life insurance policy on themselves and various family members in the amount of one thousand dollars, a lot of money in the twenties. Then when a church member died, the church would gain the one thousand dollars. I remember hearing years later that my father's program had carried our little church to great financial success. They were never hard up for cash, and the traveling preachers were always paid. I have often thought that his life-insurance program was the spark that set off our bond program some thirty years later for our Lutheran church in Grosse Pointe.

In today's world, reunions have become part of almost every high-school graduate's life. In 1984, our little school in North Dakota had its first reunion, or at least the first reunion that I was invited to.

After our school district was formed in 1888 a one-room schoolhouse was built, growing to two rooms in a few years. In 1912 the two-story, brick building where I enjoyed my total education through high school was built. In 1984 it was condemned as unsafe for children and teachers, and was torn down. So, it was decided to have not a class reunion, but a school reunion for everyone who had attended the school, even if for only one day.

In its eighty-six year history, a total of five hundred and twelve had graduated from the high school. That averages out to six per class, but I was told there was a period of seven years in the twenties when the school did not have a single graduate. In answer to my inquiry about this period, I was reminded that the twenties was one of the highest economic growth periods in our country, and all the farm boys and girls were getting married in their teens and starting up farms. Land was plentiful, and all they needed were four horses. There was evidently a relationship between the economics of our country and the education of its children.

Somewhere along the line, I received a request to handle the toast-master duties for the reunion. When Sandra and I arrived in Sanborn for the final evening of entertainment, she was given a program which stated: "Our toastmaster for the dinner and evening will be Marshall Noecker. He graduated from school in 1932 at sixteen years of age. He went east, and he done good. "

It is interesting that six hundred and fifty people attended this dinner, which was held in a large hall in a neighboring town. Many of the early graduates had died, or were too feeble to attend, so this gives an idea of the number who attended the school but did not graduate.

Naturally, one of the people I really wanted to see was Alyce La France. However, all of my inquiries about Alyce proved to no avail, and the school had a blank on her life and whereabouts. I came away disappointed as I would have dearly loved to know how Alyce spent her life and where she was.

My wife, Sandra, reminded me that her forty-fourth high school reunion was coming up, and I was not going to be invited to attend. I think she feels that I had too much fun at mine.

Another relationship that started for me in New Orleans was my friendship with Margaret and Trammell Crow. We met during World War II and continued as friends for the next fifty-six years.

In the beginning minutes of 1993, Trammell called me with an invitation for Sandra and I to join him and Margaret on their one hundred and seventy-six foot ocean-going yacht. We accepted!

We flew to Copenhagen to join the Crows, where we were guests for dinner at the home of a world famous sculptor, painter and artist. The dining table was shaped like a peanut and beautifully supplied with flowers. Each of the fifteen guests was presented with a hand-sculpted flower vase with our names personalized into the finish. This sculptor has made some beautiful life-sized and larger statues which are displayed in some of the Crow facilities in Dallas.

The next morning all fifteen of us boarded the "Michala Rose." We soon learned that the crew was made up of two captains, a navigator, map reader, two engineers, two mechanics, and nine members of the serving staff. We headed out across the North Sea to Sweden.

The Crows were experienced travelers and know how long an evening on the water could seem. So they decided ahead of time that each of their guests would provide an evening of entertainment to help fill the twenty-two day voyage.

I was chosen to open the evening programs, and since I had been told in advance, was prepared with handouts on the history of Russia and the Romanof reign. The Romanof Empire started in 1605 and it ended in 1917 when Nicholas, Alexandra, and their five children were murdered. In this period of 312 years, the Romanofs ruled the country from the days of peasantry to the days of World War 1. During this period the Romanofs took credit for all the accomplishments of Russia. Since Trammell told me in advance that I would lead off the program, I prepared a Romanof tree showing the rulers of each period of the 312 years. In addition, my tree showed many of the Romanofs who had married rulers of other European countries. It was interesting to know and to study the accomplishments of this group of Romanofs. My program was very well received, and I was surprised at the interest that our group had in the history of the Russian rulers.

We crossed the North Sea to Stockholm, them headed back to Gdansk, Poland. We crossed the Baltic Sea to Finland and returned to Russia. Our next stops were a day each in Estonia, Latvia, and Lithuania.

When our trip on the Michala Rose was over, we left the yacht at St.

Petersburg, Russia. Our group enjoyed three wonderful days in the St. Petersburg area. I knew that the city was built from scratch on a group of small islands in northern Russia as Peter the Great's door to the oceans. From my reading, I had a list of about twenty places to visit. We saw them all, including a private showing of the Faberge Room as guests of Margaret Crow.

At the Hermitage Museum, certainly an outstanding show place, we saw the world's largest piece of gold — a life-sized statue of a woman. The saddles, bridles, and other equipment on the horses were studded with diamonds, rubies, and other precious jewels. We commented that if the Russians marketed a few items from their museums, they would be one of the world's richest nations.

I had purchased tickets in the United States for Sandra and me to board the "Orient Express" in St. Petersburg and continue to Moscow. We were told this was a six-hour ride, but it took nine and one half. Our seats were not what we expected. I said to the conductor, "There must be some mistake as I purchased first class tickets and I don't think we're in the right car."

She straightened, strained her stance, threw her shoulders back and said, "Mister, in Russia everything is first class." We stayed in those seats for the rest of the nine-and-one-half-hour trip.

Homemade vodka flowed rather freely from containers similar to two-quart Mason fruit jars. The jars seemed to have no owners, and went from chair to chair with everyone taking a swig. Many passengers were asleep before we reached Moscow.

Before we left Detroit, I had bought my tickets and hired a driver to pick us up in Moscow, to drive us to our hotel and serve as guide. Sandra and I were dressed in quality clothes for our train trip, and had come on board with four rather large suitcases from our lengthy yacht trip. We were conspicuous travelers. As we approached Moscow three and one half hours behind schedule, we were afraid that our driver would not be at the station. As we pulled in, our fears multiplied. There were thousands of people milling around as you would see in Rome when the pope was to make an appearance. What would we do with our four suitcases and other hand luggage? Sandra and I were absolutely petrified.

I knew that we had told our driver to pick us up at car #12, so, we got our baggage to the platform and gazed over the crowd. I saw a man holding up a sign with a name in Russian that I could not interpret. But, in little letters at the bottom was the name "Noecker." I pushed through the crowd to reach him. After showing proper identification, he came with me over to where Sandra was guarding our suitcases. He took three and left me with a large one on wheels. He then took off, pushing people out of his way with us following. With gasping breath, Sandra said, "We'll probably never see our suitcases again." To keep up with him, I had to take the same aggressive approach, pushing people out of our way. Finally, we caught up to him. He was loading our suitcases into a Volkswagen bus. As we caught our breath I told him we were thankful that he had waited for us, and his reply was that we were his only source of income for the week, and he would have waited all night. He got a big tip.

We checked into our designated hotel and were directed to the eleventh floor. There we were greeted by two women who suggested we sit down in some big chairs while they made up our room. I commented on the fact that they had our reservation for two months and did not have the room made up. They told us they never made up a room until the guests arrived. Maybe we wouldn't show up, and the effort would be wasted. While we waited, they told us the hotel had been built in 1952 by Kruschev so that he could call in five thousand communist members from around Russia. The hotel was one of the world's largest.

The next morning we went down for breakfast, expecting a typical American hotel restaurant. Such was not the case! It was cafeteria style with a three-hundred-foot-long food display. We make the three-hundred-foot trek and viewed hundreds of choices — enough selection to satisfy any gourmet appetite. But, when we reached the end, Sandra had selected two items she deemed suitable for us to eat. I am allergic to many foods, so she had chosen hard-boiled eggs and biscuits. After eating these two items, Sandra decided that she should take hard-boiled eggs and biscuits for us each as our lunch. We had not eaten a hard-boiled egg in years, but you know our breakfast and lunch menu for the days we were in Moscow!

We walked out of the hotel into the beautiful July sunshine and made the three-block trek to the Gates of the Kremlin where we met our guide for the day. Leopold was a young man, twenty-eight, married, and with one child. He and his family lived with his parents in an apartment.

We had hit the jackpot. His English was very good. He told us his father knew that after Stalin died Russia would change. Therefore, his parents had insisted that their children learn English. (We heard the same story on our two trips to China.)

We learned enough from Leopold that day to fill a book. The Kremlin is a walled city, about three miles square and dating back hundreds of years to the Romanofs. According to Leo, the wall is eleven feet thick at the base, and forty feet high. We saw everything in the Kremlin that day, and Leo seemed to enjoy admittance to many of the private areas not available to most visitors.

As a group of three, we stood alone in the room that held Lenin's coffin and body. We were within two feet of the coffin, and it was hard to believe that his body has been lying in state since 1924. He looked so natural, it seemed like he could have stood up and talked with us. Leo also took us to Lenin's reviewing stand which is famous in pictures. I stood in Stalin's footprints to review my military power, waving and saluting to hundreds of tourists on the reviewing field. But nobody returned my greeting.

Another interesting place we visited was the avenue of Communist leaders with their life-sized statues and lists of accomplishments. We were told that Kruschev had been in the Avenue, but his statue was removed due to "uncommunistic" behavior. History will tell if his statue will ever be returned.

At noon we enjoyed our eggs and biscuits while looking at the Romanofs' castle.

Sandra had made arrangements back in the States for us to be met by a guide at our hotel on the second day. Liva arrived with a chauffeur to drive the Mercedes for a day of touring Moscow and vicinity. In eight hours you can see a lot of territory.

The sight of the 1976 Olympics was a spot that Liva enjoyed showing us. We were reminded that our president, Jimmy Carter, did not send our Olympians to this meet, which the Russians regarded as an insult.

Again, we ate our hard-boiled eggs and biscuits for lunch, this time near where wedding ceremonies were being held. Probably ten or twelve weddings were lined up for that day, with each group accompanied by relatives and friends. The brides were dressed in beautiful white gowns, and the bridegrooms in tuxes.

We also visited the university. The campus buildings were four identical towers called East, West, North, and South. If I remember correctly, Liva told us there were over one hundred thousand, yes, one hundred thousand students.

The emotions shown by Leo and Liva when we paid each them for their days of service made us realize how fortunate our American people are to enjoy our economy.

The next day we were on Air France, bound for Paris.

Nineteen

Recent History: Business

IN 1989 I WAS CHOSEN MICHIGAN'S SMALL BUSINESS PERSON OF THE YEAR by the U.S. Small Business Administration. This honor carried with it quite a few interesting appearances at public functions.

One was an invitation from President George Bush and his wife, Barbara, to be their guest at the White House. When the supporting requirements for the invitation came, they included the inclusion of two children. We chose Nicholas and Alexandra to go, and have often wondered if there were other disappointed family members. Nancy was available and went with us to the Washington, D.C. festivities, but as hard as I tried, I didn't know how to break the White House security rules to include her in that visit.

The United States Small Business Conference was held at the Hilton

Hotel in Novi, Michigan. Over one thousand people were brought together for the luncheon. I had been told that I would be introduced by Governor James Blanchard. The evening before, Sandra and I had been joking about the fact that I had made ninety-seven appearances with Governor George Romney when I was running on the Republican ticket, and therefore, I should have no trouble making my comments to this large audience. However, when Governor Blanchard introduced me the next day, my reply was, "Thank you, Governor Romney" — a slip of the tongue that brought the house down. During subsequent years when I would run into Governor Blanchard, each time he would laugh and say the best introduction he ever had was by me when I said, "Thank you, Governor Romney."

In 1993 there was a general downturn in the extrusion business, and we decided to close the Novi operation while continuing to operate our three Garden City presses. Our Novi plant sat idle for a couple years, costing us rent and other expenses. So, in the spring of 1995, we decided to move the press to Garden City. We had already put fifty-two thousand dollars into redesigning that Loewy fourteen hundred ton press, and at this time we added another twenty-eight feet to our aging oven. In August of 1995 we started the operation with the addition of this upgraded equipment, and in our opinion, it is second to none.

When we reopened our paint plant in January of 1994 after rebuilding following the fire, we needed a manager. My son, Nick, hired a young lady who was a chemical engineering graduate, a big job for a twenty-three year old. In January of 1996 she advised us that she was going to marry a young man who was working and living in Tennessee, and to have a proper marriage, he wanted her to move there. We agreed. She stayed until the wedding date in April.

Another year of college graduates were coming out that spring, and I was able to hire one or two to fill the ranks in our organization.

With our new powder coat system we are able to provide a wide range of colors to architects choosing aluminium extrusions for commercial buildings. By 1996 we found that the paint line had definitely paid off. We had been operating three shifts a day, around the clock, six days a week, and were producing some of the finest powder-coat painted materials in the country.

By 1996 we were also looking backwards as well as forward into our Noecker Fabricating department, which we started in 1990. It was growing by leaps and bounds. We have doubled volume many years, and look forward to that progression at least to the year 2000.

One of the many outstanding and interesting jobs we do in this department is the fabrication of "classic" Lionel train cars. We extrude a section of aluminum in the shape of a train car approximately two hundred feet in length, then stretch the material and cut in to the sixteen-inch lengths required for each car. We have four different projectiles that they then fabricate into seven different cars including baggage, passenger, dining, observation car, and caboose. It's a great feather in our cap to be making these cars.

In addition, we have a lot of other interesting parts we make as part of a much larger program, such as tracks for overhead cranes, flat bars for conveyors, and light shields for busses. All great and happy additions to our line of operation.

★

Recent History: Family

I WATCHED MY PARENTS RAISE MY SISTER, ME, AND MY BROTHER. ALSO, since we were a close family in rural North Dakota, I was privileged to watch my uncles and aunts raise their kids.

In raising my eight children they were not privileged to know an extended family, as we were literally 1,250 miles away from any of their cousins and aunts and uncles.

Our oldest son, Chip (a Certified Public Accountant), has raised his two daughters with his wife, Carlee, at a distance from us. They turned out wonderfully well without our able assistance.

Dana is a graduate of Southern Methodist University in Dallas, Texas and like her grandfather and her father, started out with her first job in New York City. She is engaged in the television industry.

Lindsey has just graduated from Dartmouth College and is now testing her education on the financial industry in Boston.

Carlee and Chip have just bought a villa in Florida very near to us, and therefore, we expect to see more of this family than we have in the past. Also, Chip has had his fingers in the financial market of Wall Street and has made some nice financial gains for his family.

Ann and her husband, Murray Dawson, have raised two daughters in the Chicago suburbs. Due to the proximity we have seen more of these two young ladies.

Lauren is in her third year of premedical education at Wake Forest University. Letitia is a freshman at the United States Air Force Academy in Colorado. She is also on the ski team and the soccer team of the Academy. Ann continues to be a joy in Sandra's and my life.

Our daughter Nancy and her husband, Dick Debosek, live in western Florida, near our winter vacation place. We are very proud of Nancy's accomplishments, as she is raising thoroughbred prize-winning Dutch warm blood horses. She has just returned from Amsterdam, Holland, where she purchased a filly to add to her breeding line of horses. We understand the horse made the airplane flight across the Atlantic. We don't know how to handle an airline ticket for a horse. Nancy is also pursuing a career in the real estate field.

The in-town kids get all the perks. Our son Bill is also a CPA, like his father and his older brother. Bill and Peggy live nearby. They have two outstanding children — Drew is a senior at University of Liggett School and he has just achieved membership as a National Merit Scholar finalist award. Drew plays football, soccer, and participates in debate. He is on his way to college.

Leah is a little bundle of energy, and smiles continuously. Peggy successfully runs the national Brasco bus shelter business that she and Bill own.

Our son Richard, also known as RJ in the professional field, is enjoying a successful career in the international music field as a percussionist. He makes eight tours a year — Canada, Western United States, Southern United States, Eastern United States, Europe, etc. Besides being the band leader, he manages the band and does all the booking. His mother now works for him as his publicist and as his accountant — her first career job. Richard loves to rile up his brothers by saying he is the favorite nephew of his aunts — Ruth Wilkinson, Judith Story, and Kay Wilkinson. We are his biggest fans and have grown to love the blues.

Greg married a fellow University of Michigan student, Merrilee. Together they have produced Duncan and Victoria.

Duncan plans to be an Eagle Scout, as his father and Uncle RJ achieved this status. Greg makes his quality windows by day at his window company in Detroit. At night he is a Boy Scout leader and on Sunday he is a Sunday school teacher.

Victoria is a bright bubbly first grader and loved by all. Merrilee is an enthusiastic tennis player and a great cook.

Nicholas continues his life feeling that God did not make enough hours in the day for him to accomplish all of his goals. He is now running my aluminum extrusion company and the results are successful. We are very happy to have Nick in Michigan, because wherever he is there is action and lots of fun. Usually Nick is accompanied by a good looking young lady. Nick is the son that resembles me most in every way, so I hope there are little Nickys some day soon.

Alexandra, the baby of our family, received her Masters in Business Administration from Southern Methodist University in Dallas, Texas. This degree completed thirty-five years of college education for Sandra and me.

Alex is beautiful like our other daughters and soon after graduation married Dr. Richard Ferrara. In the five years since the marriage they have blessed the family with little Richard, who is now three years old and just an outstanding young boy. We are privileged to share in his life.

Alex and Rick are expecting another baby in the very near future and when Richard was eating his lunch (including a pickle) Alex told him about the new baby. "What shall we name the baby"?" she asked Richard.

As he held up the pickle, he replied, "Pickle." We are afraid that this baby — boy or girl — is going to go through life with the name "Pickle."

For about the last ten years I have been interested in the "chunnel" — the underground tube connecting the United Kingdom to Europe. I think my interest stemmed from my friendship with Tony Speller, and the fact that I did business on both sides of the water.

In the winter of 1996, already in Europe on business, I bought tickets from Brussels — where Sandra and I had attended a performance of our son, Rick's band, *Johnnie Bassett and the Blues Insurgents* — to London via the Chunnel which had recently opened. Upon boarding, we raced across Belgium at one hundred and eighty-six miles per hour. As we approached the tunnel entrance, we slowed to one hundred and twenty, and all of the sudden, we were in complete darkness. We had expected to see a lot of interesting sights in the Chunnel, instead we had thirty-two miles of darkness. Afterwards, we spent two days in London. One evening we were guests of Tony Speller, and the other at our favorite restaurant and the theatre before flying back to Detroit and home.

Our son, Chip, received both his B.A. and M.B.A. degrees from Dartmouth. Then, on June 10, 1997, his daughter Lindsey was ready to follow in his footsteps as she graduated from Dartmouth.

Our daughter, Ann, had been with us for our first two Dartmouth graduations, and when she learned that Sandra and I were going to our third, she called and said, "I'll be there, too." It was quite surprising to both Ann and me that the format of the 1997 graduation was almost identical to the ceremonies in 1964 and 1965. As we sat in the open air, in the sunny, grassy fields, we realized that Dartmouth must be one of the most beautiful college campuses in the country. Also, Dartmouth must have some relationship to the "weather man" as we recalled that all three graduations sported the most beautiful sunshine that New England can offer.

The eight children are all on their own now.

Even though I was born and raised on the farm in North Dakota, we never had a pet in the house. My mother's philosophy was that animals belonged in barns and people belonged in the home. The only exception may have been a little chicken or bunny at Easter time. I maintained the same policy throughout my married life, until Nicholas brought us into the world of dogs.

Now we are living with two dogs in the house. When Nick was a senior at Emory University, one of his girlfriends listened to his story of a pet-deprived childhood and bought him a Red Boned Hound. The dog came home. The next year, another girl at the University of North Carolina heard the Emory dog story and proceeded to give him a North American Eskimo, with papers. So, Spike came home to join Dixie. If you wonder what happened to the two young ladies who paid for the dogs, we don't know. Nick probably does, but he won't tell us.

Sandra and I spend a portion of each year in Florida. My daily exercise is a four-mile walk on the beach every afternoon. It's a forced walk, taking sixty-one to sixty-four minutes. That is, unless I get behind one or two string bathing suits and then it takes me longer. I have only missed dinner twice!

In my opinion, every husband and wife need the principle of "prior approval" in their marriage. Whether you plan to play golf, buy a new suit, or call your brother in China, let your mate know in advance. In my case, Sandra is a very intelligent person and often modifies or improves my proposed action. We often go weeks and weeks with nary a word or feeling of discontent. Driving the car, of course, is the exception to this rule.

Self sufficiency is also important in family life. It helps when your parents have followed this rule in your childhood. In my case, life was tough in rural North Dakota Territory. Parents had their hands full making a living, and children were taught to fend for themselves. In Sandra's case, both her mother and father worked out of the home. They were strict parents, and so their four children knew the responsibilities of keeping a clean and orderly home.

This background has carried forward into our lives together.

When we step out of our night clothes, they are hung on hooks. Toothbrush and paste are returned to their proper places. The bed is made, and dirty laundry is put down the clothes chute.

We know there are a lot of couples who live in messy homes, maybe even some of our married children. But, I ask how a husband feels if his beautiful and loving wife has to stare at his dirty clothes on the floor. He would go down in her estimation. How many of us have entered a friend's automobile to see the seats and floor covered with candy wrappers, newspapers, and other items of disgust? Your mate will love you more if you keep your car clean and orderly. It takes so little time.

When all is said and done, the success of most marriages is based on a clear understanding, developed before the trip to the altar, of what a life together will entail.

I have placed prominence on both sexes in raising the children, but the mother comes first. In providing the life, the husband must be free to earn the livelihood. Money does mean a lot.

My life has certainly not been that of a normal breadwinner. I had more than one hundred and fifty aluminium window and door manufacturers in the United States, Canada, Europe, and Africa. I was often called upon to go on business trips and many times Sandra packed her bag on short notice to accompany me. She always looked upon it as benefiting my career, and in the long run, our family.

The real test of a wife and mother is the ability of all family members to get along with each other. We continue to have family gatherings and reunions with all eight of our children from our combined families. Sandra's leadership makes this possible.

Naturally, we have had our ups and downs. However, most of them have been fostered by outside happenings and people — very few by differences between us. We have been a reasonably religious family. Now that all the children are on their own, Sandra and I say our nightly dinner prayer by holding hands and looking directly into each others' eyes. It seems to say, "All is well with the world, and I love you more than ever."

Use this handy coupon for ordering.

Sanborn Press by Mail
5800 Venoy
Garden City, Mich. 48135

Please send me *He Went East and He Done Good*
1 copy @ $24.95 plus $4.50 shipping: $_____
12 copies @ $240.00 plus $12.00 shipping: $_____

Make check or money order payable to: Sanborn Press.
No C.O.D.s

Ms/Mrs/Mr: _____

Address: _____

City: _____ State: _____ Zip:_____

Use this handy coupon for ordering.

Sanborn Press by Mail
5800 Venoy
Garden City, Mich. 48135

Please send me *He Went East and He Done Good*
1 copy @ $24.95 plus $4.50 shipping: $_____
12 copies @ $240.00 plus $12.00 shipping: $_____

Make check or money order payable to: Sanborn Press.
No C.O.D.s

Ms/Mrs/Mr: _____

Address: _____

City: _____ State: _____ Zip:_____

Use this handy coupon for ordering.

Sanborn Press by Mail
5800 Venoy
Garden City, Mich. 48135

Please send me *He Went East and He Done Good*
1 copy @ $24.95 plus $4.50 shipping: $_____
12 copies @ $240.00 plus $12.00 shipping: $_____

Make check or money order payable to: Sanborn Press.
No C.O.D.s

Ms/Mrs/Mr: _____

Address: _____

City: _____ State: _____ Zip:_____